Keeping Zig
(Through thick and thin)

Kathy Seers

Woven Word

Keeping Zig

ISBN 978-1-913170-02-8

Edited by Lisa Slater

Published by
Woven Word
An Imprint of Fisher King Publishing
The Studio
Arthington Lane
Pool-in-Wharfedale
LS21 1JZ
UK

Acknowledgements

My first thanks goes to my son, David, who has been of great support to me and in helping me finance this book. Where would I be without you and your lovely family?

I would like to make a special mention to Christine at Howells Veterinary Surgery, Easingwold for taking the time to read the script I sent her and for her encouraging advice. You and your wonderful staff have helped Zig and me in so many ways, and always with the biggest welcome and a smile for us.

I would also like to make a special mention to Morag at Well Respected Canine York for taking the time to read my script. And to her and her staff for all the positive help they have been in helping me to train Zig.

To Karen and her staff at Leatham Cottage Boarding Kennels and Cattery in Stillington, York. Thank you for all the help you have been, even at short notice, when I have needed to have Zig cared for. I know of no better place to have him kennelled.

A heartfelt thanks to Tara, Holly, Gabi, Caroline with Amy and Toby, and friend Oscar, Zoe and Shane and Dave for being there when I need any of you to walk Zig for me. Where would I be without you all?

Finally, to Lisa Slater at Make Your Copy Count for her advice and work in proofreading and editing this book.

Part One: A Big Decision

For over forty years I worked in the nursing profession, during which I rarely took time off, even for illness. However, due to poor health, mainly focal dystonia (uncontrollable and painful muscle spasms) in my arms, I had to retire. The condition caused difficulty with such tasks as writing, turning pages, putting paper in an envelope and even buttering bread. To add to this, I suffered from extreme fatigue, shortness of breath; some days, I had trouble walking.

Sadly, my brother passed away. After the funeral, when driving home with my sister Maria, I decided we should stop off at the local RSPCA centre. At that time, I'd had a few months rest and my symptoms were less obvious. I did not want my mental or physical health to deteriorate, so I thought it would be a good time to adopt the dog I had waited for most of my working life.

Maria is an animal lover who had rescued dogs over the years and she was happy to join me. It was a nice diversion from the sad days we'd just been through.

I have always loved dogs. There had been a few throughout my younger years, usually strays brought home by my father.

We would have a four-legged friend to play with, and my father would have plenty of dog walks to do. I would often go with him.

We were fortunate he only ever found dogs who would never be of any harm to anyone or anything. But as gentle as they all were, every one of them was unruly, spending their days roaming the streets and coming home for food and shelter at night.

I'd never had a dog of my own to train, and there were no good examples of dog training from my family elders. Like many people in those days, it was a case of love the dog, feed the dog and let it live by its own rules. Dog training was an opportunity I don't think would have been considered even if we had heard of it.

I had in mind just the dog I wanted. It would be an older, well-trained dog who would be good company and help me keep fit in my retirement years. In turn, I would provide it with comfort and companionship.

Apart from loving the idea of owning a dog, I needed something to make sure I got out of bed and out of the house each day. Finding new employment was not an option, and without responsibilities, I am prone to being lazy. I would not only be likely to hibernate but may be in danger of stagnation. This would be especially true in the cold winter months when I would like more than ever to stay at home all day snuggled up under the warmth of the duvet.

Meeting Hobie…

Maria and I walked into the reception to join other potential adopters. We were shown to the kennel runs and started our look around at the hopefuls waiting to be adopted (although they didn't know that was what they were waiting for).

Approaching the first run, we saw a black Patterdale Terrier. I thought it so cute that I might have found my forever friend already. I stupidly put an index finger through the cage bars to coax it towards me and was promptly charged at by a small snapping dragon. I didn't know I could recoil so quickly. Lesson learned. I should not have frightened him like that, even though it was unintentional. His behaviour made me realise he was not the dog for me.

Walking past run after run, we saw Staffies, Greyhounds, Lurcher type dogs and more. None of them had the looks I wanted in a dog. I felt a little bit guilty about this as I knew every one of those dogs needed a good home. I wondered what their histories were.

We were both drawn to a run which housed a beautiful black and white Collie dog. It looked so timid, forlorn and shy. I love Collies, so my interest was piqued. However, it showed no interest in our presence and stayed in its corner avoiding eye contact.

My heart went out to it, and I wanted to be the one who was able to coax it out of its fear and depression and teach it what life was like in a loving home. The notice on the run told us of its skittish temperament and the need for an experienced dog trainer which I was not, so with a heavy heart, I moved to the next run.

There was a beautiful grey, black and white German Shepherd dog who I thought was the most beautiful dog I had ever seen. I would have liked to take him for myself but was disappointed to learn he had already been chosen for adoption. I asked if I could be given first refusal if the other adopters changed their minds, but I was informed they would definitely be taking him home.

I had given up on finding the right dog that day when, in the penultimate run, I was greeted by a puppy who was everything I was not looking for.

He was seven months old, very underweight and described as a German Shepherd dog cross.

He had the typical German Shepherd dog erect ears, was short haired with slightly longer hair to his hindquarters and tail and had a black muzzle and nose. He was described as tan or fawn in colour, but I thought he was more red-blonde. He had a large patch of red-blonde and white fur going from under his chin which gradually became pure white before it finished under his rib cage. There were little patches of white on all four paws. His legs were a little too short to complement his body length.

In my eyes, his slightly short legs were his only physical imperfection. Thin as he was, he was such a handsome boy, sporting Tim Minchin-like eyeliner. He was clearly pleased to see the two strangers standing in front of him. I fell in love with him straight away.

I immediately knew my idea of an older, well-behaved and easy-to-manage dog was about to become my biggest challenge. I ignored all the reasons for which I had been retired from work.

The name on his run read 'Hobie', but I knew I would not keep that name for him. I could hear voices in my head of people shortening it to "Ho", and there was no way any dog of mine was going to be referred to as such.

I left Maria looking at a Lurcher she had fallen for and went to find a kennel assistant to learn more about the dog I had seen. I was delighted when she took him out of the cage, put a black and green striped harness on him, and let us walk him a little way around the grounds.

As young as he was, he was an absolute dream to walk on the lead, quietly taking everything in his stride. Walking him around the grounds for a short while was enough to make me feel our history together had already begun.

We returned to the kennels to speak to the assistant again.

"I'd like to keep this dog," I said.

"Well I'd like you to go home and think about him overnight and come back tomorrow if you still feel sure," she said.

I was not willing to take the risk of going away and returning to find him gone.

"I don't need to think about him, I want to keep this dog," I said. So, she briefly went away and came back with a 'reserved' notice to put on his gate.

A troubled past…

I learnt that 'Hobie' had been found starving and neglected in a shed. He was heard whimpering by a passer-by who alerted the RSPCA, who in turn, rescued him from his plight and took him to their local vet. His body was emaciated, scoring a poor one out of ten. He had no collar or microchip.

He was given intravenous fluids to correct his dehydration, and they checked whether his emaciated condition was due to an inability to eat. Swallowing was not a problem, but he had little appetite.

A test for Parvovirus (a contagious and sometimes fatal viral infection in dogs and puppies) came back negative. However, he continued to be off his food and had poor bowel habits, so a faeces specimen for SARC (small animal routine culture) was collected which also came back negative.

All blood and faeces samples came back normal, but he was not eating and was not passing any stools. He underwent an exploratory laparotomy (an abdominal investigation to explore for foreign objects or diagnosis before an operation). They found no foreign body and nothing more than a large flaccid stomach. The wound, which left a long scar on his underside, was closed up using dissolvable stitches.

At some stage, he was given intravenous antibiotics, but I cannot be sure of the reasons for this. Although he had stopped vomiting, he had watery diarrhoea for almost two weeks following his admission to dog hospital. This may have been due to antibiotic therapy. Often when taking antibiotics, an uncomfortable and unfortunate side effect is diarrhoea.

Once he had recovered sufficiently to tolerate a normal diet and fluids, he was given the all clear for transfer to an RSPCA centre.

After hearing of his history, I was advised of the fees and rules for dog adoption. A home visit would be necessary, and any requirements for his comfort and safety would need to be fulfilled before I could take him home. This was to cost me £100.

I was so excited to know I would soon be taking this little fellow home but equally disheartened to know I could not take him with me straight away. It was like waiting for a special birthday gift.

On my return home, I excitedly visited friends nearby and phoned friends and family who lived further away to tell them my news. In general, the vibes were good, with most people saying how pleased they were I had chosen to adopt a rescue dog. Those who knew of my liking to hide away whenever the weather was bad were a little concerned I might not be up for the challenge.

I was a self-confessed fair-weather dog walker choosing to accompany friends and their dogs only if conditions were right for me. However, I knew I would take on this challenge as I do all others and would give it my full commitment.

Maria and I had no trouble deciding what to talk about that night. I was sorry she was going home to her family the next day.

Preparing for adoption...

One friend who has been of great support and encouragement almost every step of the way is Wendy. She would come to visit the kennels with me whenever she could.

She did not say at the time, but I could tell from her demeanour that she was not comfortable with dogs when she first met mine. One great give-away was the way she stopped in her tracks when she saw the size and bulk of the animal in front of her as we approached the run. It was obvious he would grow to be a big dog, but in her eyes, this playful puppy was already a dog of monstrous proportions. However, she stuck with me (or maybe behind me), and thankfully, she eventually got to know and like him and get over her fear.

I was not altogether surprised when she later told me this fear had been a lifelong problem for her. I admire her bravery and tenacity.

Each time we went to visit, we could hear his cries of excitement as we approached his run. As soon as he saw us, he would be so excited, his ears proudly erect, his bottom swinging from side to side and his tail wagging excitedly.

Suitable treats were left in a small basket attached to the outside of the runs, and we would drop one or two into his cage for him while we waited for him to be let out. We enjoyed our time walking him around the grounds and watching other adopters visiting or meeting their new forever friends.

One day when I went to visit him alone, I saw he was wearing a Buster collar. When I asked why, I was told it had been put on him because he had started nibbling at his abdominal wound; he would only need to wear it for a few days. In the meantime, he didn't seem to mind wearing it. That aside, I was allowed, as was now usual, to take him for a short walk around the grounds.

A few days later when he had the Buster collar taken off, I was in for a shock. This previously well-behaved puppy had suddenly developed the strength of a fully-grown Rottweiler and started pulling on the lead and barking very loudly at the other dogs around him. Maybe he was telling them who was in charge or perhaps he was letting them know very loudly that he was being taken out for a walk and they were not. Either way, there was not a sound from the other dogs. Once they were out of sight, he went back to being his happy self, but boy could he pull on that lead.

I was enjoying some time alone with him in the courtyard when suddenly, his tail wagging in excitement, he started jumping up and biting me anywhere he could, (although fortunately not my face). My clothing was no protection as he carried on.

"Ow, ow, ow! Stop, stop, stop!" I screamed.

I could see nobody about who could save me from my distress. Although I knew all this biting was not malicious, I did not know it was lack of socialisation that made him think this was acceptable behaviour. And it really did hurt.

I had once received a birthday present from Wendy to visit a wolf sanctuary in the South of England. It was one of the most fulfilling experiences I have ever had the pleasure to share. We had a wonderful two days learning about their practises and habits before walking with them. Afterwards, we prepared a meal which we were then allowed to watch them eat once the keepers had placed the offerings in their enclosure. We learnt that, should a certain female wolf from one of the packs jump up and place its paws on our shoulders, the safest thing to do was to stay still and upright. Although this goes against our basic instincts, the wolf would not then think you were a tasty piece of unexpected prey.

I applied this lesson to Hobie.

A volunteer driver for the charity drove into the middle of the yard, parked up and went to the back of his van to start unloading donations. People had been very generous; the van was jam-packed with towels, blankets, cages, toys, bowls and old collars and leads.

I shouted and begged him to throw something to distract the dog from its painful pursuit.

It appeared this man was rather deaf and could not hear my screams for help. However, once he was aware of my plight, he did throw a soft toy in our direction. This did the trick, and my body was released from the hell it was going through. Although my skin was not broken, it was quickly turning livid where he had caught me.

Unknown to me my distress had been witnessed by a member of staff who came out to help me. Thankfully this was not necessary by now as Hobie had calmed down and was happily chewing on his toy. It was a very bad idea to reward him for this behaviour, but I hadn't known what else I could do in such circumstances.

His behaviour had not been good, and I knew it. I asked why he would suddenly start behaving in this way. I was told that it may be because he was able to tolerate proper nourishment now and his true energy levels were returning after his stomach operation. The member of staff advised me that the centre's dog trainer/ behaviourist would be asked to come in and assess him. I waited for news of when this would be. Meanwhile, I carried on calling in to see him each day and was accompanied by a member of staff when I took him out for his exercise.

Assessment time...

On the day of the assessment, I was met by a confident and pleasant woman who told me I could make myself a cup of coffee while she was away doing her checks. I was grateful for this but getting through the wait until she returned was stomach churning. I appreciated the staff coming in and making small talk with me while they were making their drinks.

This was in the days before I knew assessors used aids such as life-sized dolls to see if the dog liked children, or a false hand on a stick to stroke the dog and interfere with its feeding time to see if it snapped. I was left wondering if he was behaving well or had bitten her and if so, was she hurt? Would she still let me take him home? You see, once a dog, even a naughty dog, has captured your heart, it has it forever.

When she returned to speak to me, she could not have been nicer. She spoke of her concerns in my keeping him and of the hard work that would have to be put in to train him. She could not promise that his biting habit could be corrected. I did not tell her dog training was new to me, but I think she may have guessed.

While she spoke, I was aware of her watching my responses and listening as I told her how responsible I would be as a dog owner, and how I intended to work with her on his worrisome issues.

I knew I was taking a big risk, but I was up for the challenge. Something inside was telling me he deserved that chance.

I must have looked worried because she said to me; "Don't worry love, I'm not going to tell you that you can't keep him."

My tension visibly eased once those words were spoken.

After further discussion, she seemed satisfied with my good intentions but did ask if I was going to be able to control him as he got older. He was a big puppy who was going to grow into a big, strong dog. I was silently thinking, 'I hope so,' but I vocally assured her. She left me, seemingly happy that I would carry out my duties to the best of my ability. Further training classes and home training sessions were to be arranged.

Awaiting the day of his adoption, pending a positive result from the home visit, I was enjoying a coffee in the company of friends who were talking about whatever was on their minds.

My mind was on a new name for Hobie. I made several suggestions, which were all turned down. As my friends carried on with their chats, I was busy going through the alphabet trying to think of an alternative name. Having got all the way to the letter 'Z' I interrupted their talk.

"Zig! How about Zig?"

This name was met with approval. I had hit the jackpot and was now going to adopt a dog who would be named Zig. I told the staff at the RSPCA centre of Hobie's name change when I next went to visit.

Before the day of the home visit, I met the lady who would be doing the assessments. She, like the rest of the staff, was very pleasant.

"Will Zig be able to come on the home visit too?" I asked. I had been thinking about his untrained behaviour and was wondering how he would behave outside the kennel environment without so many dog savvy staff around. The answer to my question was that it might upset him to be taken out only to be brought straight back to kennels again.

On the day of the visit, I welcomed the lady into my home. As we sat at the kitchen table with a hot drink, we discussed where Zig would be staying.

Initially, he would be limited to the kitchen where we sat, but once he had settled in, he would have the freedom to roam the house.

What safety and comfort would I be providing for him? Would I be leaving him alone when I went out? I showed her where his bed would be and where his water and food bowls were going to be kept. I gave her the name of the vets' practice I intended to use once the adoption was complete.

I lived in a rural community and was a car driver, so there were plenty of country walks and parks for us to visit. Leaving him home alone was something I had not intended to do. I had no paid or voluntary employment, so I intended to take him with me wherever I could.

This lady definitely had my dog's interest and well-being at heart. I contentedly listened to her as she told me about the German Shepherd dogs she had rescued and now took to schools and homes as 'pat dogs' and 'therapy dogs.' I wondered when I would be able to do such a lovely thing with Zig.

All went well with his placement provisions indoors, but the garden did hold a few problems. I would have to make sure it was dog secure. I needed to put six-foot high fencing where the natural hedging had not grown. I also needed to replace my three-foot gate with a six-foot gate to ensure he could not escape. Such was my ignorance of homing a dog; I did not know gardens had to be dog secure.

I asked why the fencing and gate would have to be so high. I thought it might be so he did not annoy our close neighbours. But no, it was because a dog of his size and build might be able to clear anything lower. I had witnessed on several occasions next door's pregnant spaniel jumping over to my side of the three-foot wooden garden fence with ease. I was agog in wonder and awe when I first saw her do this. There's no way I could have done that while I was pregnant. I thought this might be any dogs limit and was surprised to learn some dogs could jump up as high as six foot. I have since seen Zig in action and know this to be true.

These issues were easily rectified with the help of good friends and neighbours. One who put up the fencing for me at 'mates' rates. The other, a good friend, who donated, fitted and secured the gate for me. Both men willingly stood in front of their work while I took the photographic evidence needed to show that I had made the garden as secure as requested. I showed the pictures to the RSPCA staff who thought them satisfactory.

I was eager and impatient to get my dog home to where I lived in the rural village of Crayke in North Yorkshire. This busy and prosperous community, set in the Howardian Hills, is known as an area of outstanding natural beauty. Its main income comes from farming, though there are a number of residents who commute to and from work every day. It boasts a church, a castle, a thriving pub and a primary school.

I would watch as owners passed by my house with their

dogs. Every dog either walking nicely on a lead or walking just as nicely beside their owner without one. I wondered how long it would be before I could walk out so comfortably with my dog. I longed for the day to come.

Once I had been given the all clear after the home visit, I spent some happy hours shopping for things Zig would need. I chose the plushest bed I could find that was adequate for a large sized dog, though it would be quite some time before he would fill it. It had a deep filled soft cushioning inside and was white with black edging. It was the least sensible of colours to choose for my dog, but there were no other colour options for this bed, so I bought it anyway. When I got it home, it fitted perfectly in the space I had set out for it.

A new collar and lead, dog bowls, brushes, toys and more would all be needed, and I delighted in buying them, just as I had enjoyed buying for my children years earlier. I loved being a mum and providing them with all they needed, and now I loved doing the same for Zig. I was like an expectant mother laying out the nursery in readiness for her baby's arrival, putting the food and drinking bowls in their place in front of the utility room and screwing in hooks on the other side to hide and hang his collar and lead on. My old kitchen bin was useful to keep his brushes, cloths, towels, poo bags and toys in. Another one was bought to keep his dried food in. These fitted nicely in the space.

Treats were placed in a large jar near the kitchen window; he would know whenever the lid was taken off that he would be getting a treat. I bought the food he needed from the RSPCA centre along with dog chews, and more poo bags and toys. I knew by now it was not sensible to suddenly change a dog's usual diet as it can cause problems with the digestive tract.

In-house training at the kennels continued for the short time he was still there. He would be taken to the courtyard with the trainer and me. He was being taught that paying attention to me and learning what was being asked of him paid dividends in the form of tasty treats.

A kennel assistant would then be asked to stand some distance away with a well-behaved dog who would obligingly stand still beside her and take no notice of Zig while he was pulling at his lead and barking, paying more attention to the dog than he was to me. Occasionally he would be still for long enough to earn a treat.

If the RSPCA staff could bring out any number of quiet, well-behaved dogs, why did my dog have to be such a noisy mouth organ? We would need a lot more of this training when I took him home.

As if to prove he was a dog who would need a lot of training, he bit one of the kennel staff; not seriously, but she felt it. She was so good and forgiving about it telling me not to worry and that it was better he bit her than anyone outside. I think she was being very charitable. This worried me and made me wonder again if I would really be taking him home.

All that was left to do before I took him home was his neutering and microchipping which happened in the next few days and healed up without any problems.

The wait is over...

On 14th October 2012, I was finally able to take Zig home as my own dog. He was now seven and a half months old and putting weight on nicely.

The RSPCA centre was having an open day, and parking in the car park was difficult, so I had to park outside the grounds. I managed to get the attention of one of the busier than usual staff and told her I had come to collect Zig. She took me to reception then went to get him from his run while I waited with the staff and received and signed the necessary paperwork and paid for his adoption.

The £100 I paid got his adoption papers, insurance for a further four weeks, immunisations, flea and worm treatments and records, neutering and microchipping. Not to forget the veterinary care and operations, the in-house assessments, training and home visit that had already taken place. I was also told there would be a follow-up visit in three months to check on how we were doing.

He was now officially handed over to me, so I took him to the front of reception to wait for the help I needed to get to the car with him and the goods I had bought. He was not going to go quietly. He barked and barked until we left the building, leaving visitors wondering why on earth I was taking such a noisy handful of a dog home with me.

I opened the back door of the car to put away the goods I had bought and then opened the car boot for Zig to jump in. Not a chance! He had not a clue of how to do this or what I was asking of him. After several attempts to get him to do as I bid, the assistant picked him up and put him into the boot.

"Just this once," she said. Now our adventures were truly about to begin.

Part Two: Training Zig

You will now read of the not too few difficulties I have had with Zig since his adoption. At times you will perhaps wonder why I should choose to keep him, if you are not doing so already. He has on occasion, had me at my wits' end, not least for his innate hunting instincts, something I knew nothing about before taking him home. But I have worked very hard with him in my goal to calm and socialise him.

If I write a good account of our time together, you should come to understand just why I chose to keep him and how I have turned him into a happy, friendly, loving, protective and safe dog to be around. Zig has worked very hard too.

Settling in...

On the drive home, I spoke non-stop the entire way in an attempt to reassure Zig.

"You're coming home with me now Zig, and I'm going to love and look after you, and we will be best friends forever."

While my voice was shaking with excitement, he needed none of this assurance as he very contentedly sat in the car boot looking out of the window at all we passed.

Once home, I took him to the back door and opened it to let him into his forever home. I was expecting no manners from him and thought he would run in ahead of me, giving no regard to my safety, but I was wrong. He stood at the bottom step and waited for me to go in first, then he had to be encouraged to come inside.

I could hardly hold back my delight at the way he was wagging his tail as he excitedly sniffed around. Once he was satisfied that he had investigated the kitchen thoroughly, he made his way to the plush new bed I had bought for him and claimed it with a look that said; 'I'm the King of the Castle'.

I had also bought a large dog cage for him to escape to if he was misbehaving or feeling worried in the early days when we had visitors. I padded out the bottom of it with an old duvet which he took to quite nicely. As its gate was left open all day, it quickly became a place of refuge and peace for him. He very quickly understood the 'go to bed' command. He would be shut in there at night, especially in the early days to prevent possible destruction while I was not with him. Sometimes he preferred the cage to his comfy bed.

Next, he needed a toilet break and a good sniff around the garden. Before I let him out, I filled his bowl with fresh water which he lapped up with gusto; what a messy drinker. He left puddles of water across the floor from his bowl up to and on the mat at the back door. The neighbouring dogs on either side let us know they were aware of this newcomer's presence by barking in unison. I doubt Zig had ever had the freedom to run off the lead and sniff the ground around him before that day because he ignored the neighbouring dogs.

I phoned the insurance company and registered him as my dog at my address and took him for his registration and initial check-up at the vets. He was instantly at ease with the vet and new environment and enjoyed all the attention he was getting.

For his first appointment, he was seen by one of the partners. As she was doing her routine health checks, he was busily hard-mouthing her arm. She did not seem to mind this, at least she was tolerating it very well, but she did let me know how important it was to get him out of this habit. I knew she was right. However, her forearm was suiting him as a good chew for now.

Once home again, I phoned to register his microchip to my address and let them know his name was now Zig.

The trainer had advised that I should be Zig's only company until he had settled in with me. However, I did have one visitor who came with a bumper gift pack for him.

'Maybe just one visitor won't harm,' I thought to myself. Zig smelling treats came forward and sat before her as she got one in readiness for him. As he was receiving it, she said, "He's beautiful Kathy." I already had no doubt about this but was pleased with her confirmation and smiled in acknowledgement.

At teatime, as advised, I ate before he did. He came and sat beside me at the table in the hope I would share with him. Giving him no eye contact as I ate, he quickly realised he was getting nothing so went back to his bed. I called him over to his feeding bowl when it was his mealtime and put it down in front of him. He was truly unimpressed.

Standing before it he looked around at me as if to say, 'Am I really supposed to eat this?' I did not know why he wasn't eating because this was the same food as he had been given at the kennels. Maybe he had never smelt food as good as mine before and was hoping for some of that too.

When the trainer next visited, she explained this was his way of saying; 'Is this all Mum? Is there nothing better?' This did not last nor did I change his diet for him.

A minor setback...

Though I knew not to allow visitors to the house just yet, I did not realise that meant I was not to take him out either. The following morning, I took him out to have a sniff around the immediate area and was met with approval from the school children waiting for their bus. He tugged at his lead in an effort to meet them and pick up their scent.

Later, I took him for a short walk just outside the village and was finding it hard to control him. The drivers in their cars were pulling up in close succession one after another clearly thinking he was going to run into the road. Thankfully it is a small village and no more than six cars, which appeared together, passed us by.

That afternoon, as I was watching him play in the garden, my neighbour looked over the wall to ask about Zig. We were quickly in conversation about all things dog. It was decided that one of her dogs would come to my garden to see how they got on together. I had forgotten already about the advice to have no visitors.

Although he was a boisterous, untrained dog, it never

occurred to me that he might not play nicely. I really was naïve.

It was a nice meeting; Zig let the other dog take the lead with the introductions and we were quickly comfortable with their play.

After only a short time my neighbour was happy to leave the dogs playing and returned to her own house. I decided to go indoors and make myself a cup of coffee.

I had just switched the kettle on when I heard a yelp followed by whimpering coming from one of the dogs. I dashed outside, wondering if one of the dogs had been injured and was surprised to learn it was Zig, the bigger dog, who was hurt. He was standing in almost the same place I had left him when I went indoors and was looking very sad.

My neighbour walked back into the garden also wondering what had happened. She was worried that her dog had hurt my dog and I was relieved that my dog had not hurt her dog.

Once she knew it was Zig who had been hurt, she was embarrassed and apologetic. However, there was no need for her to worry as there clearly had been no bad blood between them nor was there any visible sign of a fracas having occurred. While Zig was standing still on the lawn, her dog was passively sniffing its way around the garden.

Zig was clearly in pain, but I hoped it would not be for too long and he would be back to his playful self very soon. I could not help but notice how good natured he was being even though he was in such pain. When he tried to walk, he limped at his right shoulder and kept lifting his paw. When he tried to get up the steps to the back door, he was unable to do so and started whimpering again, so I had to lift him into the house. I watched and pampered him and let him rest while talking soothing nonsense to him, hoping he would soon be up and about again. However, I could see his pain was not going to go away, so in less than twenty-four hours after his first visit, it was time for us to return to the vets.

Examination confirmed the pain in his right shoulder but little else. This time he was not chewing at the vet's arm. He was prescribed a course of anti-inflammatory medication which he was to have once a day with food. We went home with instructions that he was to rest and only be taken out for toilet breaks. An appointment was arranged for him to be seen again after the weekend. I gave him his medicine as prescribed, but he was still in pain throughout the next forty-eight hours and was finding it difficult to get comfortable. Because he was in so much pain, I allowed him to stay in the front room with me.

I called Alice, my friend from the village, to let her know that I had taken Zig to the vets because he had an injury already. She was at my door within minutes. She and her family have a dog of their own who they treat and love as one of their family, so I knew she would share my concerns and be just the company I needed.

While she sat on my sofa with one leg crossed over the other and a hot drink in hand, Zig struggled over to her and rested his muzzle on the top of her elevated foot. His efforts earned him some gentle finger stroking along the length of his snout. Now they were friends.

When he was unable to bear the pain of standing any

more, or he had just had enough attention, he quietly limped back to his comfy place. Once she had gone home, I helped him out to the garden to do his toileting. Because he was already a clean dog and knew not to use the house as a toilet, I made sure I lifted him every few hours, so that he could relieve himself. I fed him and gave him plenty of water which he struggled to get to. I brought it to him if he really could not get to it.

The return visit to the vets on the Monday suggested some lessening of his shoulder pain when resting but soreness on movement and deep manipulation. Again, we went home with instructions to continue the anti-inflammatories and strict house rest.

Although examination by the vet suggested a little reduction in his pain levels, he was still very sore and no less lame, so I continued to carry him up and down the steps when he needed to go out, but I encouraged him to walk to the door before lifting him. He was very stoic for such a young dog.

Before the next weekend, I received a phone call from the vets enquiring after Zig's condition. I explained that he was now limping on his hind leg too. This was likely to be compensatory to the initial shoulder injury. I was advised to bring him back for a further appointment the next day and to starve him from midnight in readiness for x-rays and examination under general anaesthetic.

On examination, before the anaesthetic, it could clearly be seen he was still in pain and lame and had slight muscle wastage to the affected shoulder and some damage to the tendons. X-rays of his hips were also taken while he was still under anaesthetic.

When his results came back, I was not expecting to be told he has bilateral hip dysplasia, a condition in which the ball-shaped joint at the top of the femur does not fit properly into the socket of the hip joint. The left side is noticeably more affected than the right. There was inflammation of the long bones and perhaps a greenstick fracture of the femur.

I looked at his x-rays with the head vet who showed me where the abnormalities were and talked me through the problems he would likely have as an older dog. She asked me if he had been neutered and when I said 'Yes' she said this was a good thing as problems like his were not a good thing to pass on. A second opinion from a veterinary orthopaedic specialist was advised. I agreed to this. It was time to contact the insurance company again and talk them through the events which had taken place over the past seven to ten days. Fortunately, because he was registered with them before he left the RSPCA, they were happy to pay out the insurance needed for his treatment.

I continued his anti-inflammatory treatment and rest. He was now sporting a big bald patch where he had been shaved before the examination under anaesthetic. This got him plenty of sympathy from friends who came to visit.

The result from the orthopaedic specialist confirmed a healed greenstick fracture of the femur which had repaired at a slightly twisted angle causing altering to the knee and hip mechanics. He also diagnosed panosteitis (painful inflammation of the shafts of the long bones). This condition, which is also known as growing pains, is thankfully not a lifelong problem, but it can last for as long as eighteen months. It has a greater prevalence in larger dogs such as Zig, who is part German Shepherd.

Conservative treatment was continued as per my wishes, and a return visit was scheduled for four weeks ahead. Thankfully, with the help of anti-inflammatories and the professional care of the vets and practice nurses, that unhappy start to our lives together is a thing of the past. We keep an eye on how his hip dysplasia is progressing. So far it is giving him no problems.

Bouncing back...

On a professional level, I love Zig's vets. They have seen us through a lot and shown us the greatest of care and professionalism whenever they have been needed. All the staff have such a welcome for us when we arrive whether it's for a simple weight check, health check, yearly injections or something serious. Zig is always eager to go in to greet them as though they are long lost family. He shows no fear.

When he had properly recovered from his injury and invasive procedures, he went back to living in the kitchen and making use of his cage. Not least because he was back to his habit of biting and jumping up again. Plus, he had recovered enough to enjoy playtime in the garden.

I was back to dealing with his lack of socialisation which was still profound; together we had a lot to learn. It was bruised limbs for Wendy and me until I managed to get him out of this nasty habit.

Though Wendy tolerated much and bravely helped me where she could with his training when she was at my house, it was me who bore the brunt of his playful but painful biting and jumping. My limbs remained livid and sore. Friends were so worried about me because of his behaviour and the thought he might seriously hurt me, they suggested I took him back to the RSPCA. In truth, while I was determined to keep him, I was somewhat worried myself.

When I took him back to the RSPCA for his final doses of immunisations, I told one of the Staff about what he was doing, but she told me I needed to persevere with him. Not satisfied with that reply I showed my wounds to another staff member. She looked horrified when she saw the red and blue bruising on my arms and had me show them to yet another member of staff who said much the same as the first lady I had spoken to.

I took Zig back home, hoping with all my heart that we would get through this, but worried in case it got worse. I felt like I was dealing with a delinquent child who should be in a house of correction, but I could not give up on him. There was also that gut instinct that we would get to our good place together. Besides, I do not like to admit defeat.

A bigger worry for me was that if I took him back to the kennels because of his biting, even if in play, it would be a death sentence for him. He was not a well-behaved dog, but he deserved better than that, a chance of a happy life and to grow and learn how to improve. A chance to be a puppy who played until his heart's content and to grow old happily knowing he is loved. How could I even think of risking him being euthanised just because he did not know the difference between safe and unsafe play? It was up to me to learn how to correct this.

But as determined as I was, I was to make a series of mistakes from which I had a lot to learn on the way.

So much for problems inside the house. Getting him into the car for our trips out was an ordeal for me. Having to lift him into the boot for each visit to the vets had already told me he must learn how to do this. It was an instruction he took his time in learning. Even throwing treats to the back of the boot to encourage him, did not give him the know-how to jump in. Maybe he thought he wasn't allowed to jump in.

However, once he had mastered it, he thought it was his given right to jump into the back of any open car boot.

I would sometimes be driving to a chosen destination when he would have me jumping in my seat with fright if I drove him past horses on the roads. He would bark long and loud until we passed them. He would make an almighty noise at the back of my car and would not stop until they were out of sight. Thankfully, I was always wearing a seatbelt and managed to keep control of the steering wheel. After a while, I knew to expect this and would ready myself for it. I got used to distracting him when I saw them up ahead. Gradually, some idle chat was often all that was needed to distract his attention. Sometimes he would be sleeping so I could drive by without a problem, although I would still warn passengers to be aware if I saw horses up ahead.

By this time, I knew he was a better-behaved dog off lead than he was on it. However, I always asked people who had their dogs on a lead if it was okay to let him free and would explain why. On one occasion when I was about to walk him past a very large Alsatian type dog, keeping our distance, I did as usual and put Zig on the lead before explaining to the young woman how much better behaved he was if not leashed. Having done so, I asked if she was happy if we walked past without the lead attached. She gave a very definite yes. But once we had passed, Zig having behaved impeccably, the woman turned and shouted at me saying I was lucky her dog did not kill mine and I was a fool not to have had him on his lead.

I could not believe what I was hearing. After the great explanation I had given her and asking if she was happy about what I was doing, she said this. I responded by saying; "Were you not listening to a word I said? I have just spent time explaining to you what I intended to do, and you gave me clear permission to do so." With that, she left me, and we went our separate ways. The rest of the walk was uneventful, but the incident left a sour taste in my mouth.

Training...

It was time for the dog trainer/ behaviourist to start her home visits. I waited for her arrival one morning, with all the gear and no idea what would happen.

Zig greeted her with the usual enthusiasm he has for all people, which she ignored until he settled down. She explained to me how I should be turning my back on him and giving him no eye contact at all until he stopped jumping. Then I should very quickly reward his good behaviour by giving him a treat and the attention he was after. If he started jumping up again, I was to turn my back on him and ignore him as before. Eventually, he settled.

As we were sitting at the kitchen table having hot drinks, Zig remained settled; she was throwing small cubes of cheese to him at regular intervals while she was talking to me. This kept him quiet and nicely behaved. It was a useful trick to use in future. He likes cheese and very quickly got the idea of waiting quietly so that treats would continue to come his way.

When I told her that I had not been able to get him to behave like that, she put me at ease by telling me things that go wrong for an owner will go right for a trainer. How right she was.

When we moved away from the table, he was quick to follow and start his unfavourable behaviour again. For this, I was advised to leave him in the kitchen and close the door behind me for ten to twenty seconds before going back in as if nothing had happened. As soon as he started again, I was to leave again and repeat this action until he eventually got the message that jumping up and nipping was not going to work in his favour.

I told her I was having trouble putting his collar on him so once he had settled again, she showed me how to introduce it, briefly showing it to him before passing a treat through it. Gradually she brought it closer to his face and further over his head and kept it there for an increasing length of time, each time giving him a treat before he finally allowed her to put it on him. I tried this but found it so time-consuming, I started to approach him from the back with the collar ready and swiftly put it around his neck. In fairness, he wasn't as hyper about it by now. Once he was used to it, he would put his snout to the collar for himself, so there was no need for me to sneak up on him from behind. It is as if he knows he needs his hat and coat on before going outside, and if I am too slow about it, he nudges my leg as though saying, 'Get on with it'.

For fun and light relief, I was shown some tricks to teach him, so he would not get bored and would learn how to get more treats for good behaviour. He enjoyed learning, was quick to catch on and the plentiful treats that came his way were never refused. Treats at this stage were to be up to two-thirds of his daily diet.

Before she left us, I asked her if she had an idea of what breed he might be crossed with. Taking a good look at him she said, "Maybe some Staffy. But that doesn't matter does it?" Having gotten to know him and thinking of him as an extra limb by now, I told her it didn't. But secretly I was thinking about how I did not want a Staffy. Walking around the kennels looking at all the Staffies waiting to be adopted, I had particularly chosen not to get one. It was a bit of a shock when she told me that. I have since been told on lots of occasions that people can see Alsatian or Malinois Shepherd, Staffy, Labrador and Ridgeback in him. It is easy for me to see the Alsatian/Malinois Shepherd in him with his erect ears, long black muzzle and long body. The wide forehead, wrinkly grin, big chest and shorter legs of a Staffy are also obvious. The only thing Labrador I see in him is his killer tail;

it's so strong he could knock a child over with it. As for the Ridgeback, no matter how often I am told people can see the breed in him I cannot. Whatever is in him he is a lovely dog.

I think he may have done well as a working dog, having the satisfaction of getting tired after a day's work well done. I would sometimes wish a farmer, or maybe a customs officer would offer to take him to work with them for the day to tire him out mentally and physically. I wondered if I was being cruel by keeping him as my dog when I could never give him the exercise or training he needs. I try to make up for him not reaching his potential by making sure he has two hours of exercise and walking every day.

Following the trainer's advice, I went shopping for brain teaser toys. One of which was a dispenser ball which I filled with dried food for his breakfast. I watched and laughed as he chased it around the kitchen floor, chewing each biscuit as it dropped out. He thought it great fun. I wondered how all this activity while eating a meal did not make him sick. This and the other educational toys I bought for him served well. Like a child after a hard morning at nursery, he would fall asleep for an hour or so after breakfast.

He earned lots of cheese cubes and meaty dog treats before the next training session. He never tired of cheese or running around the kitchen working out how to get food from the dispenser. Unfortunately, as a puppy, he had a sensitive stomach, and I soon had very loose and stinky stools to deal with. It would not be unusual for him to empty his bowels six times a day. I was grateful he was already such a clean dog with his toilet habits and always waited until he was outside.

When the trainer came back the week after, she said I need not worry about this as I could cut back on treats as he responded to his training. I did not need to worry about how many treats or how much food he had daily as he still had a considerable amount of weight to gain.

I watched lots of YouTube videos for ideas about how to teach him more tricks. My kitchen looked like a mini dog training school with chairs in odd places and flattened cardboard boxes placed across the table legs to stop him sneaking through until he knew what I wanted him to do. Before long I had him walking backwards, sitting, standing and circling left and right for me. He enjoyed every moment that my attention was focused on him. Plus, when distracted in fun, he had no need or want to jump up and bite.

Master of destruction...

It was six months before the lady from the RSPCA came to do the follow-up visit, and I was beginning to have doubts about her returning, but she did. We sat at the kitchen table with the usual hot drinks while we went through all that had happened since his arrival home, how I was managing him and whether he seemed settled and happy.

All was well except for the incident when he had to go to the vets with his injury and him being diagnosed with hip dysplasia. I told her I was not happy at not being told of this before his adoption, explaining that this condition was one of the easiest to suspect and an examination and an x-ray would quickly have confirmed it. That aside, all was fine. It was a good meeting made better by her telling Zig what a lucky dog he was to have come to live in a house like this. There were smiles of joy and gratitude from me.

Destroying the kitchen was his favourite new pastime, so I spent many hours in there correcting him with click and treat training. He still needed to be watched, and I would occasionally forget this at my own expense.

Wendy and I were enjoying the warmth from a roaring coal fire while concentrating on a game of Scrabble one evening while Zig was keeping warm on his plush bed near the hearth. Concentrating on our game, we were blissfully unaware of what he was doing with the bed that had almost broken the bank when I purchased it for him. Wendy saw it first. When I turned to see what he was up to there was little sign of him. He had chewed a large portion of the edging apart and was buried up to his ankles digging himself further into the white cushioning as he was sending out piles of it at the other end and onto the floor. I had to coax him out of it before shovelling up the mess and disposing of it. I considered repairing it, but the tears were so jagged, and the material so threadbare in places, that it was not worth keeping.

I have since bought several other supposedly dog proof beds for him, but he tears into them in no time, so I have given up buying them now. He has the use of all the chairs and beds throughout the house, so he hardly lacks in comfort. He seems to respect that anything above floor level is not for chewing.

At some stage amongst all this, it was Bonfire night. I was at Alice's house, and she was talking to me about the worries she had for her dog that evening. Her dog did not like the event at all and would run to the smallest place in the house looking for safety. Alice would have to comfort her the whole time while the poor dog quaked in its skin.

This got me wondering about Zig, and I started to worry too. I watched and waited for the first sign of fireworks orbiting towards the sky and listened out for whistles and bangs. I already had great concerns about other animals living outside, over or underground. Bonfire Night is a horrible time for them.

Pssst. Wheeew. Boom and bang they went as the colours lit up the night sky. I waited for a reaction from Zig in readiness to protect him. I had a cosy blanket ready for him to snuggle into while we sat together as I pacified him. I made sure he had done his business beforehand so there would be no accidents in the house.

Nothing! He carried on as normal while flashes, whistles and loud noises invaded the night sky. He ate, drank and slept as usual. I now think that if he were a human, he would have been a Marine or a circus entertainer as a human cannonball. You could send him out wearing a bomb and he would not flinch. However, turn the page of a newspaper over in a quiet room, then you would see him startle.

My middle sister Detta (family pet name) came to visit me and meet Zig. I was in the kitchen washing dishes after dinner when I heard her screaming "Gerroff!"

I quickly went to check on what he was doing, hoping he was just a bit too playful for her, but really, I knew that he would be nipping at her legs. Once I had made sure she was okay, I took Zig to the kitchen and left him to calm down while we had a cup of coffee. She was now another concerned person wondering what the hell I was thinking of adopting such a crazy dog.

Misdemeanour now forgiven, we had fun later as I taught him to pick up his toy and bring it to me and to place his paw on top of the cup that had the treat in it.

She also witnessed the destruction he had made to the kitchen. I learnt too late that taking a trip to the loo or answering a phone call out of his sight was too long for him to be left alone. Table and chair legs were chewed, the lino was ripped apart, and the new skirtings I'd had fitted were chewed into, along with the wallpaper. I had fully intended to get new lino once he was settled and no longer destructive, but I had not realised just how pleased I would be to have waited.

With two people temporarily available to keep an eye on him he was allowed in the front room. Keep an eye on him? That was a joke. You only had to take your eyes off him to sneeze and it would give him enough time to get his mouth around something he shouldn't have. He made short work of the television remote control and the telephone handset. The handset, though an unwanted expense, was easy enough to replace, but I was to wait weeks for a replacement remote control. This dog sure was high maintenance.

Teaching him tricks was fun and paying dividends when he was engrossed, but when I wanted to relax, he would start jumping up and biting again. I worked hard at leaving the kitchen and closing the door behind me for the ten to twenty seconds suggested by the trainer, but this was to no avail, and weeks of this work was tiring me to the point of exhaustion. So, I started leaving him in his cage in the kitchen for five to ten minutes at a time, and when I returned, he would be suitably chastised. Although this did not stop the problems straight away, he did get the message more quickly, and finally, this problem was at an end. At last, I could make a hot drink or a meal without the fear of him biting. Wendy could safely come and stay over too if she wanted to. It was good to watch my skin return to its normal colour and my friends could worry about me less.

Incidentally, I was given the name and number of a horse whisperer I was told worked well with dogs too. In desperation, I invited him to come and meet Zig in the hope of getting some good advice from him. He was a very amiable and patient man who ignored Zig's territorial barking and stood unmoving at the kitchen door until we had a quiet dog in our presence. One piece of advice he gave me was to try and keep my feet still as I was being bitten around my ankles from under the kitchen table. The idea was that if Zig got no response, he would quickly lose interest. His words brought back memories of my weekend with the wolves. I noted it was very much easier for him to sit quietly while he was wearing strong ankle covering boots. I liked him a lot. He made a few more visits to us after his day's work, but when it was time for me to offer payment, he refused to take it.

A few months later, I called him to ask if he would like to come and see the changes in Zig's behaviour. He was delighted by this invite and further delighted with Zig when they met again. He told me that he had never heard from anyone he had helped before and it meant a lot to him to be asked back.

Having gotten Zig over the biting and jumping up phase, I now had to teach him not to put his paws on the table or worktops to steal food. This dog did not only know how to earn his treats; he knew how to steal them too.

He quickly learned the value of not doing this and to wait with all four paws on the ground until his food was put down for him. Now I can leave food anywhere, except on the floor, and he knows not to touch it. He does like to watch me eating, which I know is not allowed in the rule books, but I don't mind so long as he doesn't sit in front of me and drool. If he does, I simply tell him to go away and he obeys, knowing he will always get the last small bite of whatever I am eating.

He still had a lot of weight to put on but was eating well, filling out nicely and was in good physical fitness. I would sometimes take him to the vets just for a weigh in and be happy with his progress.

Taking me for a walk...

We practised his walking to heel up and down the garden with the trainer. Fortunately, I had a long garden, so there was plenty of room to practice this. As expected, the training always went well with the trainer. It went well when it was Zig and me alone in the garden, but once we got beyond the gate, anything we had learned together he completely abandoned.

While he wanted to pull me along like a dray horse, I was sure I did not want him to do that. Trying to teach him how to walk nicely was to him just another way to earn treats. He had me trained in giving them out in no time as I would mistakenly throw them down before waiting to see if he was following the training regime. I had been told to let him have a treat that had been offered, even if I had done the wrong thing. It was my mistake not his, so I kept up with this practice.

My inability to teach him this skill has cost me dearly in the different types of harnesses and leads I was advised to try. All were good in their own way, but they did not work out for me. He had chewed through his first two leads, so I bought him one with chain links which attached to his soft collar. This did not go down well, but I had to use it until he knew not to chew through the fabric. The chain itself was never directly attached to him. I do not like choke chains around a dog's neck myself. Once he knew not to chew, I did stop using them.

One idea with the harnesses was to try one with a double ended lead which would attach to the top and bottom of the harness so that I could pull his back end toward me. This was supposed to encourage him to walk next to me with his whole body in a straight line and control his pulling. This failed me too.

I tried at least another three, but he had a powerful chest and shoulders. I still found it too much of a struggle to control him if he was keen to get anywhere. When I met a farmer on one of our walks, he suggested I tried a noseband-to-collar type of restraint which would control him from his head, thereby giving him less force from his shoulders when I was trying to direct him. This is not perfect for us either, but I find it better for controlling him than the other alternatives, and it's much more manageable for me. I wish we could try these products out for a day or two to see whether they are right for us before we buy them. I was pleased when I managed to get some money back selling them on at a car boot sale.

He does not like the noseband; he thoroughly hates it. But if he insists on pulling, I need to keep it on him, and I do take it off with his lead when he is at play and when we are walking home afterwards because he is too tired to pull by then. Getting him to walk to heel on the lead has been my biggest failure. Still, I try.

When out walking, especially if we were walking along the verges of a road going out of the village, he would pull on his lead doing his best to chase traffic. On one or two occasions, in his eagerness to pursue a moving vehicle, he would turn his face towards me, shake his head and pull himself free of his collar. Fortunately, when he did this, his reaction was akin to finding himself walking the streets without his trousers on. In apparent shock, he would come back to me and wait while I put it back on. Feeling better dressed and more secure, he happily went back to pulling.

This collar was clearly not doing the job it was intended for. It became more obvious when, unbeknown to me, it had fallen off his neck. I had left him swimming in a small stream as I went ahead, knowing he would soon follow. The first I knew of it was when I turned to check on his whereabouts and saw him with it in his mouth before he dropped it in front of me. I could not believe how clever he was being. I was relieved too because I was on my way to check for sheep in a field that I was hoping we could walk across. This was a lovely field for him to have an extra five minutes of playtime in if it was empty. Today was a lucky day, but I would have had difficulty controlling him if his collar had been lost and he saw them.

I had reported to the trainer about his eagerness to chase traffic, so we all practised walking together near a busy road and he did very well. However, these walks were on a wide path and a grass verge away from the road. It was much more difficult to keep him in check in the village where the roads and verges are a lot narrower. I took the training tips on board and used them to the best of my ability. In fairness to the trainer, I never did tell her how much I was still struggling when he was near traffic in the village.

Soon after I bought him a costly new collar with a strong Velcro fastening which promised to last a lifetime. He lost this in some hedging and nettles in his first week of wearing it. Where was my clever dog now? Try as I did to get him to find it, he could not or would not do so. Why did he only decide to show how smart he can be when wearing his cheaper collar? He had no problem playing among the nettles when he was wearing it, so why would he not go back in now?

Late in the evenings I would take him to the back garden for his final toilet call and give him five minutes play chasing after the ball. He learnt to drop it, so I would throw it again after just once showing him what I wanted him to do. I have such a clever dog. Why then can't I teach him to walk to heel on the lead? Not such a clever me, I guess.

Keeping him within the confines of the garden instead of taking him out for a walk last thing meant I was free of his pulling. And it was all he needed before we settled in for the night.

Even though he was a clean dog, in the early days if more than one person came to visit at a time, he would become excitable and a little nervous and would sometimes wet the floor. I felt sorry for him when this happened as he would look so ashamed as he slunk away. There would never be any punishment for this, and as he became more comfortable with visitors to the house this behaviour stopped. He still got excited when they came, and I would have to remind them not to pay him any attention until he had settled down. Sometimes I felt as though I was teaching them more than him. Once he had settled down and knew he was getting no more input, he would devour his stuffed toys. I am guessing this would be his way of dealing with his stress. I wondered what had happened to him in the shed he had been found in.

He is a naturally dominant character who did not like me correcting him and would often give a single bark at me in defiance whenever I instructed or corrected him. There was never any sign of aggression shown, but I knew when I was being told off. He was quite comical to watch as he walked back to his cage determined to have the last word.

Out and about…

Once he had learnt to accept who was boss, his gentler nature was apparent for all to see. He loved to people watch from the window or the gate and often they would come over to say 'Hello' to him and stroke behind his ears. He was eating well, sleeping well and behaving well.

Now I had managed to improve his behaviour indoors, I allowed him to explore the rest of the house with me. I had not intended to leave him alone anywhere apart from the kitchen, but it was nice letting him investigate.

I stood at the bottom of the stairs waiting for him to finish sniffing around the hallway until he noticed where I was. As he had done when I first brought him home, he waited for me to go up the stairs first. I felt a gentle pressure from his snout and paws as he followed me too closely. He did the same when we were coming back down, and I was worried he might knock me over. Because of my concerns, I decided to teach him to walk up and down them ahead of me. I feel safer with this.

The time had come for him to go for some private training lessons in the classroom. We practised meeting and greeting stuffed animals, again using the click and treat method. I had to work at keeping his attention on me as a stuffed dog or sheep would be brought into view. There were many circuits of walking him a little nearer to them before being taken back to the original starting place when he pulled on the lead again. Slowly we were able to get closer as he was learning not to pull. Though he never did get right up to the replicas to sniff at them. Despite our hard work and good intentions in the classroom, and me trying hard to get him to behave on the lead when outdoors, he forgot all this training when he came close to the real thing.

It was several months before he was allowed into the training classes with other dogs. Every week I would be shown teaching strategies by a trainer, and then I would be left to carry on in a room where he was out of view of others and them out of view of him. He was very good at keeping his attention on me when there was nothing to distract him, but if his interest was piqued, sometimes treats did not work. On one occasion he bolted through the doorway of the room to join the other dogs. His intention was not to join them in training, he wanted to play but would have been a very disruptive influence.

If we were doing outdoor training, we would be on a separate grassed area doing what we had to do. As with the approaching a stuffed animal training, I was taught to do this outside with Zig by keeping his attention on what training we were doing and slowly getting closer until he was on the same grassed area as the other dogs.

Eventually, he was let into classes with the other dogs to continue basic training, good behaviour and learn some agility. He was allowed to join other dogs in outside activities too. This slow process was an absolute necessity until he had learned life was not all about play and was willing and able to take instructions from me, with or without distractions.

In our first full autumn together, I would take him out to exercise in a closed field close to home. We had many visits there until one day, after looking around as usual and before letting him off his lead, he spied something over the hill that I had not. Cows.

With the speed of a racehorse, he took off without warning. I worried in case he got kicked or chased by them. If a cow had gone in for the attack, I would not expect Zig to come out alive. He returned after circling around and barking at them a few times as they showed no interest in him whatsoever. There would likely have been a very different outcome if there had been calves in the field too. It stopped our visits there for a long time, at least until I had a willing partner to accompany me as I passed them with Zig on the lead. I am a "townie" not a country girl and am not comfortable in such close proximity to cattle.

When not running or rolling about in a resting field, he would delight in sniffing out and picking up cow pats. Why do they like to do this?

"Yuk, how disgusting. Must you really do that? Put it down now! Your face is never going to come near my face again. Ever."

'But Mum this is fun'.

"No, put it down now!"

My words would go unheeded as he ran off with these disgusting lumps of faeces, hoping for a game of cow pat Frisbee.

That field was not the only field we would walk across, and at times they would be wet and treacherous. This was no deterrent to Zig; the more mud he had to roll in the better he liked it. I would be grateful to get to a beck where he could swim and clean himself of the mud he had loaded himself with. He loved these five or ten minutes of play time and was showing himself to be a strong swimmer and lover of water.

By this time, people who once took their dogs away at the mere sight of him were more relaxed in his presence. They realised that even though he was a boisterous dog, he had learned not to bulldoze his way between owners and other dogs. He knew now, with reprimands and some resulting nips from other dogs this was not acceptable behaviour. He loved it when anyone stopped and talked to us and gave him a good rub around his ears and under his chin. He would wait patiently at my side until it was time to move on.

This autumn was a handy time for me to watch and learn how to get him to stay and wait. I had become aware of a man training his dog in a field. Unbeknown to him, I picked up some useful training tips and practised them with Zig in the same field. He loved this training; I think it was because when I let him come to me after waiting as instructed, he would have enough space to stretch his legs at a good pace before reaching me again. At first, I would simply walk around him and if he stayed, he would get his treat or the ball thrown for him. It did not take too much time before I was able to walk a good distance away from him.

Sometimes I would take him to a nearby park where there would be no unwanted distractions for him. By unwanted distractions I mean livestock. He loved to go there and run around and seemed to have a smile on his face as he enjoyed playing with other dogs. It lifted my spirits to see him like this, especially when people would say how happy he looked. I would mentally give myself a little pat on the back when I heard this because to me it was confirmation of how well we were doing together. Inwardly I smiled to myself because I knew he would never need worry again about ill-treatment or where his food and water was coming from. He could put his total trust in me. Plus, while he was enjoying playing with other dogs, it strengthened his socialisation skills. He was doing just fine.

Around this time there was a small culture festival in town.

A big bus was brought in for children to play on or do drawings and paintings; a small theatre of actors and storytellers worked from local shops and pubs, and singers and comedy entertainers shared their talents for a short time from an empty bath used as a stage placed in the Market Square. I liked the idea of this and decided to be part of some of the audiences. I took Zig along with me simply because I did not like to go out without him. The best of the entertainment for me was a youth choir who were performing songs from Les Misérables. I knew some of these songs well because at the time I was a member of a choir out of town. Spectators from the audience were invited to stand in and sing with them. I happily stood at one end of the front row with Zig sitting next to me. So far, so good.

The young conductor stood at the front of his choir ready to bring and blend in all the voices on cue. It started smoothly, but we had hardly got to the second line of the first song when from my left came the high pitched sound of a howling wolf.

"Arh whoooooooo, arh whoooooo, arh whooooo."

It was immediately evident he was not going to stop. Although I appreciated his sweet serenade, all he was doing for the choir was spoiling months of hard work perfecting their concert. Part of me shamefully admits to seeing the funny side of this. The conductor did not. Out of deserved respect, I took us away from the scene as quickly as I could and listened from a distance far enough away to keep Zig's howling at bay. When I went back the next year, I made sure not to take him with me. I have not heard him practising his high notes since that day.

Winter...

I was appreciating changes in nature I had never taken much notice of before, the different trees and hedgerows that were growing around us, such as the Rowan, Beech and Hawthorn; even the humble privet hedges grew pretty white flowers. I have always been aware that flora flourished and died throughout the year but not quite when. I was learning now what time of year the harvests would be cropped and when the fields would be tilled and their crops sewed. I would be amazed to see how quickly new green growth would follow. Cows and sheep would finish grazing in the fields, so there were more areas for Zig to run and chase after his ball, or just have a good old sniff around. When the large round hay bales were in the fields, I would love putting a tennis ball or a treat on top of one of them, so he would climb up to get his reward. I don't know if it was me watching, or him having such fun, that was enjoyed the most.

It was not long before winter was upon us. A season I have always hated. Looking out of the windows would be enough to make me imagine freezing to death. I don't even like to see snow on Christmas cards. Bah humbug, I am.

Walking Zig once the snow turns to ice is a very precarious activity because of his lead pulling. I would be better off having him pull me along in a sledge than him trying to get me to free skate.

This is the time of year I would really like to confine myself to the warmth of my bed. I had to put such ideas out of my head now as I had a dog who loved and needed plenty of exercise. Out of necessity, I have toughened up against the elements since adopting him, though I still dislike the cold, rain or snow.

I was to discover that as much as I hated winter, he was in his heaven. The first time I took him out and let him off the lead to play in a field of snow I watched how he loved to chase through it after a ball. When he took a break from that, he rolled onto his back, and with all four legs in the air, he shamelessly twisted and turned in the cold white cushioning as if to do an energetic version of a doggy snow angel. I was delighted by his antics and soon forgot I was cold.

One of his favourite pastimes was to dig large holes in the lawn, and he especially loved it if the soil was wet. Click, treat and gentle reprimands soon got him out of this activity, at least in the garden. Before success with this training, there were deep skid marks and mud mounds aplenty leaving what used to be a lawn looking like a mole heaven. A ready-made estate for them to navigate. All planned out and executed for them by Zig.

Another cause of having such a poor excuse for a garden was next door's apple tree. The branches hung over into my garden and dropped many an unwanted piece of fruit onto my lawn. I love most fresh fruits and eat lots, but I am not so fond of them if they have been adulterated in any way, such as being stewed and put into a pie, so these apples were nothing but waste to me. This tree was the bane of my life, but because it had been there for such a long time and never failed to give a good apple fall, I respected it's right to be there.

I said 'No' to the tree owners when they asked me if I wanted them to cut it down. Instead, they had it pollarded which helped for the year, but it was back to unwanted apples the next year. I left some of the best ones out for passers-by to help themselves to, but very few were taken. Bending down to pick them up was too much for my lower spine, shoulders and arms to bear. I would leave plenty of the best under the hedge for the wildlife and throw the rest from the far end of the garden to near the gate using the ball thrower. Zig loved chasing after them, and as they landed, there would be another one for him to run after again and again. I never let him eat any of them, and he never tried to. Play was enough reward for him. This way I would save my back and shoulders from impending pain and stiffness and have the apples close enough that I could sit myself down on a low collapsible stool and use the ball thrower to draw them in towards me. I could then put them in a bucket before decanting them into the garden bin.

We continued our walks, enjoying and discovering new routes to trek. One such route took us to the back of a house where a path had been fenced off for walkers. As the winter rain continued to fall, walking here was becoming more difficult, but it was part of a regular and enjoyable walk for us.

One cold, wet day, being very pleased with the thought of soon being home and clean and dry again, I was suddenly almost knee high in a thick muddy puddle and was unable to free myself. I was stuck fast in cold watery mud, which caused me to fall forward and bury my hands and forearms into the mire too. Mud on my glasses added to my struggle. Zig could not in any way be held responsible as he was off the lead at the time. Being off the lead meant my plight merely meant more play time for Zig. I eventually managed to free myself and walk home with saturating mud adding an extra stone in weight to my body. When we got home, it was me who needed the greater hosing down. Thankfully, the landowner rerouted the path, thereby avoiding further mishap and misery.

If vanity is your middle name, do not get yourself an active dog who loves mud. Do not walk in places you are likely to come a cropper in if you step into deep muddy puddles either.

Bath time...

As winter was leaving us, I was enjoying the good times we were having, and walks were mostly pleasant. The snowdrops were plentiful and in full bloom and crocuses were showing promise of the wonderful parade and variety of colours they were soon to become. The land was still a muddy mess and could be hard to walk through. It did not help that I had adopted a hippo who was disguised as a dog. He would take any chance he could to wallow in a mud bath. And every time he did, it was as if it was a whole new experience for him. He has never learned that the consequence of mud play is shower or bath time.

He hates being hosed down or bathed. Even having him tethered on a short lead near the back door while the deed was done would be difficult. I'd struggle to shower and clean him as he moved around trying to escape his watery fate. This would always cause me great back and shoulder ache. Even so, it was a long time before I decided I would try cleaning him in the warmer bathroom, away from the chills of the cold weather. I thought that kneeling on the floor beside the bath to clean him would be less painful to my back, but no. While I ran the bath, I would have him wait in the kitchen while I placed old towels and sheets along the hall, up the stairs and on the landing to the bathroom door. He did not like it when he was first introduced to the idea of getting into the bath, so I had to help him in. Until then he had come to accept it as a large pool of water to drink from before I got into it. Now whatever way I choose to shampoo him he begrudgingly accepts it, even getting himself in and out of the bath.

This regular wet weather chore is especially tough; he is hard work to clean because mud sticks fast to him. I can never get him clean with just a quick rub down. A good wash with at least two shampoo repeats is always needed. I am no winner either on these occasions. Shampooing him outside using the hose means staying out in the cold and growing colder. I'd try towel drying him outside to get rid of the excess water, but then he would step into the kitchen and shake off more excess water than I thought possible. As I cleaned walls, cupboards and floor, my kitchen looked more like a muddy outhouse than part of the home I was struggling to keep warm and cosy looking. If I shampooed him in the bathroom, I would have the bath, sink, toilet, tiles and floor to clean before gathering up the never-ending mountains of dirty towels and sheets I'd now have to wash and dry.

I know other dog owners face these issues, but the more

sensible ones have thought to get themselves a smaller dog or dogs who are lighter in weight and can easily fit into a sink if needs be. Zig is a big dog to clean.

Having to get myself clean and changed out of my dirty clothes before we can settle into a warm house adds to the troubles. I take him out three times a day but two walks are shorter and away from muddy areas, so it is only once a day that he gets really dirty.

I have always determined that his playtime is his playtime and if he is not doing anything to cause harm, he can do as he pleases for that hour or so. An advantage to this is training after he has had a good play always pays dividends.

Adventures...

Living in a rural community often means passing sheep, cows and horses. Despite all the effort we had put into training Zig to deal with approaching animals in a classroom environment, it was no use when it came to the real McCoy.

It would have been a good idea to have had Zig at the home visit and to take him for a walk around the nearby farmland to meet these animals before he came home with me. If this had been done, at least I would have known what I would have to cope with and maybe gained some strategies in advance to help me teach him and control him. I might even have changed my mind about adopting him over this. It was one thing to take a chance on his behaviour improving when it was my skin he was biting, quite another if he attacked farm livestock.

He was not like the dogs who so placidly walked through

the village and passed all other animals without a second glance. He would bark and lunge, getting all four paws off the ground at the first sign of livestock. I came to rely heavily on clicker training for this, and it was not easy teaching him to walk nicely as we passed them. For a time, I did everything I could to avoid walking him around such areas. I was grateful for the dog-friendly park we frequented nearby and getting us there by car was easy. It was also good for Zig to keep meeting lots of dogs and owners he now knew, and to have plenty of occasions to tire himself out through play.

Once he had enough play, he would sometimes enjoy a walk through the small woods which are to one side of the park. It was months before I would dare take him in there because I was afraid I might meet people on horses. Also, I did not know how big this wood was or if I would get us lost. Any of my family or friends will attest to my diabolical sense of direction. I only have to do a 45-degree turn to lose the sense of where I am. When looking at the wood from the park, I had the uneasy feeling Frodo and friends had portrayed when approaching Fangorn Forest.

After asking many people with dogs how long it would take to walk through, and whether there would ever be any horses about, I eventually dared to investigate. The woods, I was told, could take up to an hour to wander through and ended at a council footpath on the other side from where we were standing. Riders were not allowed to take their horses through any part of the woods.

With trepidation, I walked us through in an almost straight line from one side to the other. My nerves were only calmed once we had reached the other side and were able to walk along the narrow council road. All the time, I was looking out for horses. In case of trouble, I kept Zig on his lead. After the experiences I had of asking people if horses were in the stables near home, I was not about to take anybody at their word; I had to find this out for myself. Suddenly I remembered how, in certain areas, sheep are left to roam freely in fields, on the roadside, or in wooded areas, and now I was in a state of new paranoia in case we should come across them too. Once I reminded myself, he was on his lead, I calmed down a little.

I would only dare to take a diverted route if I had someone with me to navigate. Even then, I was uncomfortable until I felt we were back on 'terra firma'. I know we were already on terra firma, but for a time when I walked through these woods, they seemed like an alien land. I know all roads lead to Rome so to speak, but I was not going to feel happy and secure until I returned to the 'Rome' I was familiar with.

One day, when halfway through our walk, I met and chatted with a lady I felt confident walking with. Suddenly, she said to me, "I'm going to take my dog this way now, you need to go that way to get back to the park again." Saying nothing, I let her walk away as I wondered how I was going to find my way out. Zig had no such sense of foreboding and enjoyed himself while I worried.

I have never yet managed to spend as much as an hour walking around these woods, nor have there ever been any horses. Now I wonder why I ever worried. The only reason for concern is trying not to disturb the occasional young courting couple looking for a place to escape to undisturbed. Zig loves going in there to sniff out the many wonderous smells on offer that dogs love. It was also often drier than the park in the wet weather and they are a wonderful refuge from the heat in the summer months.

We were walking near the edge of a fully-grown wheat field on a lovely sunny day when we almost bumped into a Hare. Surprisingly Zig did not see this as prey. He just sat on his hind legs with the lead loosely attached as we all stood looking at each other. I have no doubt that the animal was at least uncertain, if not terrified, but I was happily transfixed by the sight standing upright before me. The splendour of this beautiful creature, it's russet red and grey coat, large impressive amber eyes and proud over long ears kept me captivated. Zig too was stopped in his tracks just looking at it until it leapt further away into the wheat. Even when it started running Zig showed no inclination to chase it. I wished I'd had my camera with me to show how close we all were, but I doubt I would have thought to use it if I had done. I made up for the lack of visual imagery by relating the event in great detail to anyone who cared to listen.

Hunter instinct...

Feeling rather sure of myself as a dog owner by now, I was enjoying leaving Zig off his lead on our longer walks but would be sure to put it back on at the first sign of livestock large or small. However, one day, I was in trouble. We were approaching a local farm where I knew hens were freely left to roam. I could see no signs of them so keeping my eyes peeled, we continued our walk with him off the lead.

Out they came. It was like 'schools out' with no parental control and they did not know to look for signs of danger. I had no chance at all to harness Zig as he chased after them. My desperate calls for him to stop and come back to me were unheard as he went after his chosen prey. As expected, one poor hen met her end as a sacrifice to a not yet properly trained dog and an owner not yet as savvy as she thought she was. The pursuit was quick, and the hen was killed in little time. Once he had accomplished his quest, he dropped it like an unwanted trophy, and without as much as a sniff at it, he ran back to me.

I hated what he had done and that I had not been fast enough or sensible enough to avert this unnecessary death of an innocent animal.

With a feeling of personal loss and my heart racing thirty to the dozen, I walked us to the farmhouse to confess to whoever was at home what had just happened and offer to pay for the cost of their murdered hen. As I walked the short distance, my mind was full of concern about the possibility that this particular hen might have been a family favourite, maybe even the children's pet. I hoped I would not have to deal with the threat of having my dog put to sleep. I know he had been very, very naughty but as angry as I was, I worried for him. That he was born to hunt is not his fault. And we had come a long way with training and socialisation in our time together.

There was no one at home, which in one way had me breathing a sigh of relief. In another, it was only prolonging the agony until the day I had to face the music. It took a week of me visiting the house at different times of day before I got an answer to my door knocking. Meanwhile, I worried about the cost of replacing the poor hen. I am not a country girl and truly did not know whether replacing it would cost £1, £1,000 or more. Was it just your average hen or was it perhaps a rare breed of great value? Since childhood, I have always owned up to my sins however harsh the consequences, but I could not help wondering what the financial impact might be on my small pension pot. Still, I kept thinking 'my dog did it, I am responsible for my dog and his actions; I just have to be ready to pay out however much it might be'. But would listening to my conscience cause me to become bankrupt? I dreaded finding out.

Finally, a lady and two children answered the door. I asked if I could have a quiet word with her without the children being present. They dutifully walked away at their mother's request. Left alone with her I was trying to control my heartbeat as I confessed.

"I'm sorry to tell you it was my dog who killed your white hen last week." Phew, I'd said it.

"Oh, don't worry about that. It was an old hen; I'm just happy we don't have a fox," she said.

I thanked her for her understanding. Having got that part of the ordeal over with I now broached the subject of financial remuneration for the loss of the hen. Praying, as I had been doing all week, it would not be too costly, while resigning myself to the knowledge I would be paying up however much it might be.

"Don't worry about it, it didn't cost much anyway," I was

told.

We parted company with me promising to buy free-range eggs from her in future. Guilt over what had happened was what I had to live with now. As I drove home, my heart, though relieved, was still pounding uncomfortably. I did not sleep well that night.

Following that incident, teaching him to walk past the hens without going in for the attack was included in his further training. He did very well, and I was further impressed with him when horses, sheep and a young bull were introduced to a paddock nearby, and he would nicely walk by them, all for a treat or six. Sometimes I would take him to have a closer look at these animals, and he would be so well behaved I thought I had the dog of all dogs. My part of the training was to put him on the lead before reaching these farm buildings whether I could see hens or not.

A short time later, I got to know the elderly man who lived in one of the farmhouses associated with the free-range hens. Because I would often take Zig walking along the same path, I would sometimes be invited in for a cup of coffee. I found him an easy man to chat with and listen to as he talked to me about what was going on with the cattle and land around us. He would also reminisce to me about his childhood and married years. As we were enjoying our coffees, and he plied me with cake and biscuits, Zig would play rough and tumble with the family's beautiful black Labrador dog. They hit it off instantly and were a good match for each other as they raced around one of the resting fields, or in the spacious dog-secure garden if the hens were roaming free away from the site they were playing on.

Our bond...

Spring had taken over from winter and the daffodils were coming up to join the crocuses, their strong green leaves growing proud for all to see, but their flower heads still hiding. Daffodils are not amongst my favourite flowers, but I loved the pleasure they would give me as I walked past them and wondered at their ability to regrow and crowd the long verges of our most frequented walks. How much nicer they are growing in their natural state and habitat than being cut off and put in a vase. This was another of nature's beauties I had taken for granted before adopting Zig. I now love watching the flora and fauna changing and growing around me as old seasons pass and new ones begin.

My back garden, though showing all the signs of floral rejuvenation, was still being overshadowed by the deep cavernous holes Zig had dug into what used to be a lawn. However, his behaviour had improved here too. A sharp 'leave it' was enough to stop him in his tracks. There was a lot of work to be done before I would be able to get it to its former glory, but I was able to keep it in reasonable repair from then on.

Worries about his previous destructive behaviour in the house were at an end, apart from what had become the inevitable destruction to any bed I bought for him. Though he still liked taking and crunching on the coal from the scuttle and leaving it wherever he pleased on the lino.

Having, at great expense, had repairs made to the damage

he had once left in his wake, I was now able to leave him alone in the house for a while, safe in the knowledge my home would still be intact on my return. I was even able to sell his cage.

I was happy with our progress, apart from the lead pulling. He was also expecting less in the way off treats now. I was enjoying the freedom and bond between us.

Although I had always sworn that he would never be allowed on the furniture or my bed, my convictions dissolved all too quickly. One evening as I was on the sofa and he was on the carpet, I felt the need to be next to him. I knew that I'd have to go down to him if I were to get what I wanted. As I lay beside him stroking his fur and massaging under his chin and around his ears, I felt the warmth of his body and the evenness of his breathing. It was so comforting and hypnotic. The floor was not the most comfortable place for me, so it was no time at all before I would regularly invite him onto the sofa to share cuddles. No biting, no hard mouthing, just a perfect peace between us.

One evening I remember him lying at the foot of my bed as I went to sleep. When morning came, he was laid facing me with his head on the opposite pillow, his snout almost touching my nose. I must have disturbed him because he woke and lifted his head to have a look around. Once he had sufficiently assured himself that all was safe with his surroundings, he closed his eyes and returned to snoozing as if he had every right to be there. I quietly laughed at this and watched him for a short while before my own eyes began to close again. That was it; he was now a regular guest on my bed, me under the duvet and him on top. The radiating warmth from his body keeps me snug in the cold weather.

As lovely as all this sofa and bed sharing is, a few words of advice to those of you who are thinking of doing the same. If you have a dog who sheds hair, it and it's undercoat gets everywhere. Keeping it under control is an endless chore. When I decided to adopt Zig, I was pleased about his short-haired coat. I thought short hair meant less shedding. Not true. He sheds his coat all year round, and I brush him very regularly. The undercoat is soft and lush to the touch and comes out in handfuls. As plentiful as this is, it is the easiest to scoop up and throw away or to throw out for nesting birds. It is the coarse top hair that is more difficult to rid from furniture, carpets and clothing. Despite my efforts to control it, he still manages to invade the house with it.

Accident...

I was happy by now to leave him to roam about the garden when I went out. I felt sad at the thought of having to lock him in the house whenever I was going out without him. I did not have to feel sad for long though as it was only a short time later when I saw him jumping up on his hind legs and opening the back door, something I did not know he could do. He had obviously been watching me and had taught himself how to do it; clever, clever dog. In the meantime, I had bought a padlock for the gate and from then on, he was free once again to enjoy the garden in my absence. He now opens all the doors in the house if he wants to get into a particular room, so I have had to teach him to close them again. He does well.

Walking home from Alice and Tom's house one pleasant afternoon after enjoying a leisurely cup of coffee and a chat, I was met outside my house by a few neighbours. They were waiting to tell me that Zig had run into the road and been knocked down by a car before running back into the garden, but he seemed to be okay. How he escaped from beyond the gate was a mystery as I had made sure I had closed it properly before I left.

After briefly listening to and thanking the neighbours I went to check on him. I found him hiding behind some bushes at the far end of the garden. I slowly approached him and coaxed him out. He was happy to see me and remained so while I checked him over. All seemed well, so I took him out to see the neighbours and show them he was alright. I thanked them for their concerns before we parted company.

As he seemed to have suffered no physical traumas from his confrontation with the car, I decided to go ahead with our afternoon walk, and he seemed ready for it.

He jumped into the boot of the car with his usual excitement and ease, and as I drove us to a dog park out of the area, he sat happily in the back. Our destination was about a twenty-minute drive. I parked up, and once he had his lead on, I let him jump out of the car. He was happily wagging his tail as we arrived at the park and I let him off his lead.

I was taken aback when he met a dog he knew, and instead of making his usual greeting he started barking and intimidating it. There was no real attack, but he tormented the dog and, as he approached, he nipped at it's hair several times. No skin was broken. This behaviour was surprising, as he had never acted in this way toward another dog before; it was not acceptable. Unfortunately, dogs can be difficult to catch when in action and I was finding it difficult to grab his collar to take him away.

The owner of the other dog who did nothing to move his dog out of the way said to me, "If your dog attacks my dog again, I'll get him by the collar and kill him." Getting him by the collar was what I was trying to do and was all that was needed to put an end to this intimidation, so why did he not try to do that or take his own dog away rather than threatening to kill my dog? As upset as I was, I understood his anger and concern as I put myself in this man's place.

Upset with what the man had said, I said nothing and carried on with my efforts to catch my dog. When I managed it, Zig was reprimanded, though not too severely as I believe his reaction to this dog was due to the fright he had half an hour earlier. I think his message was 'I don't want you to come near me, so I am warning you to stay away,' so to speak. I wished I had had the sense to know I should have kept him at home. I had not thought about mental trauma. I think he was defending himself against what he perceived as an apparent danger after the knock he'd had from the car.

The other dog was a gentle soul, older and quite a bit bigger than Zig at the time. Once I had removed us from the situation, I was ready to take him back to the car. Whatever the reason for his behaviour, it was not going to be rewarded by a good playtime. Besides, it was obvious to me now that he needed rest time, not play time.

Before we left, I turned to the man to apologise and explain what had happened earlier, but my words fell on hostile ears. 'Not a good time to talk,' I thought.

It was a few days before we went back to that park. When we did, I saw the man getting his dog out of his car, so I approached him again to explain what had happened days earlier. I thought it would help him realise there would be no further intimidation from Zig. But he stone-faced me and took his dog away. It was such a shame as these dogs had got on well. In the early days, I had come to appreciate this man's dog for the help he had been with Zig's socialisation. Being an older and well-socialised dog, he was a good teacher.

I was standing in front of this man weeks later, while watching Zig playing with other dogs and behaving very well, when I heard him say, "That dog is called Ziggy, and he's vicious."

I wanted to turn to him and shout; 'His name is Zig, not Ziggy, and stop maligning my dog. As you can see, he is playing nicely and being no trouble at all. If you had cared to listen to me when I tried to let you know of the trauma he had been through only half an hour earlier, you would perhaps understand the reason for his unusual behaviour on that day'.

Instead, I held my tongue and kept my patience in check. I knew my dog had behaved badly at the time, and that was unacceptable, but it was out of character and had not been repeated. I knew he was upset for his dog, but there had been no harm done. This man has never chosen to accept my apology or listen to my reasoning for Zig's behaviour, so I keep well away if we are in the park at the same time.

Stables...

There were stables close to where we lived, and for a long time, they were empty, so I thought they had been abandoned. I had got very comfortable with this until one day, two horses had been stabled in them. Zig realised this before I did and with the eagerness and strength of a lion, he suddenly lunged towards them. All his paws left the ground, and I had a great struggle to get him away while he continued his pursuit towards the unphased horses. Getting him back on his lead was an ordeal which left me out of breath and weary. Even when attached to his collar again he acted as if he was still running free. I was already used to being pulled along by him, but this took his strength to another level. Next time we passed by, he would be on his lead, and I would hopefully have regained full upper body strength and be better prepared to control him. I thought I had better start using the noseband again. The treats would have to be extra good to sort this problem out. This dog was definitely born to hunt.

I loved letting him off the lead on our walks and recall was much improved, that was when there was no prey about. I would ask people coming from the opposite direction if the horses were in the stables, and if they said 'No' I would leave him free. This was another mistake. Never trust people to be truly vigilant, especially if they are not dog owners. Luckily, now I knew of the possibility they would be there I would see them before Zig did and divert his attention in time to put his lead and noseband back on him and practise more click and treat training.

Approaching the stables while out with Alice and her dog, a rather proud and contented looking horse was relaxing with its head poking outside the upper half of the stable door. I gave the usual wide berth while using click and treat distractions but this time it was too much for Zig, even though I had meaty treats at the ready. In pulling away from me one of his hind legs caught mine and caused me to fall the full length of my body. This loosened my grip on his lead, allowing him to break away and bark and jump up at the horse. Thankfully the height of the lower door was sufficient to stop him reaching the horse who, like the cows he chased in the field months earlier, did not give a damn.

Before she could come to my aid, I managed to compose myself and tried coaxing him away with a sizeable piece of cooked chicken. The success was all his when he ran back to me and snatched it from my hand before returning to his worrying pursuit. Was I never going to get this dog trained and safe to walk out with? It seemed as soon as I had control of one issue, another one was there ready to challenge me.

For a time, my surveillance of the area was hyper-vigilant whenever we passed those stables. This problem took weeks to overcome, but with grit and determination, he became less excitable and I was aware of the safe distance required to pass by. This was achieved with no more than the expectation of a few tasty treats.

It was not only horses in stables that were a problem. Horseback riders would sometimes add to my problems in keeping him under control. There were times when I would be kept helplessly waiting and struggling to keep control of him while they would stop and let their horse graze or have conversations with people they met rather than moving a safe distance away for us all. If I could have moved us away, I would have but there is not always a gap in a hedge of a side road to slip into. However, most riders being aware of my needs understood the struggles I was having and what I was trying to do and would thank me for keeping him away while they passed. As we got to know each other, I knew they would wait at a sensible distance while I got him to a safe place and kept him distracted with treats.

You may be thinking that Zig gets a lot of treats and think I have encouraged him into a lifelong struggle with obesity, but I always reduce his meal time feeds in accordance to the number of treats he gets. He is in peak physical condition. I only wish I could be as strict with myself. However, all the walking I do with him has resulted in my losing a good stone in weight. I hope that is of some encouragement to the humans who dutifully walk their dogs miles each day to keep them fit.

The stables were eventually demolished, so at certain times of year when we took that route, I was able to let him run free. He would love it when the crops had been harvested and the land was free for him to roam before it was tilled and new crops planted. He was happy too when the corn crops, which were spread wide apart, grew high and he could weave his way through them without damaging the plants. He was only allowed to do this once these strong plants were well established and he would do no harm. Any seedlings, young crops or those which grew close together were no-go areas and he would be kept on his lead. If we had a wide path to walk on, I would keep him in check by calling him so he would be distracted and get on the path again.

April showers...

Along came April and with it, the expected showers. Down, down, down came the rain. It was like a fight for domination between Zeus and Indra. The roads were awash, the rain winning the war against drainage systems unable to cope in their struggle. People's gardens, farm fields and their crops were drowning in the weight of water.

Whatever the weather, if you have an active dog like Zig, you have to take it out daily for long walks and plenty of exercise.

The roads and the fields were still flooded, but when the rain temporarily stopped, I would take him out for his afternoon walk. This is always his longest walk of the day.

Because there had been no rainfall since early morning, I decided to wear waterproof boots that came just above my ankles. Though the path was still very wet, we were enjoying our time out. Sheep were far enough away that there would not be any chasing from Zig; he was wallowing in the fun of splashing in the plentiful puddles.

I walked through a particularly long puddle that I thought not to be too deep, but I was wrong. My boots filled with icy cold water. It was so cold I wanted to be out of those boots as quickly as possible. I headed towards a nearby low garden wall as my feet and lower legs ached to the point of cramp. I sat down and tried to take off my muddy boots to empty them of the water and wring out my socks. However, there was a vacuum between my feet and the boots. I struggled for what seemed like forever in my attempts to pull them off. My arms and legs ached from the effort, and I got fatigued and out of breath. Zig was quite happy and useless to my plight as he enjoyed extra time in the mud and puddles. At last the sound of a loud squelch of air entering the vacuum, my efforts allowed me to free a foot. But I had to rest to catch my breath and let the aching in my arms and legs subside before I could get on with freeing the other foot. By now I had got used to the cold temperature. With water free boots and wrung out socks I continued our walk home. The thought of having to get us both clean and dry at the end of our walk was purgatory. We still had a mile to go and the rest of the journey was miserable for me, but there was no trouble from Zig. Good boy.

Never before or since has getting Zig cleaned and getting me out of wet clothes, and into a nice hot bath and pyjamas, felt so good.

I longed for summer to arrive when we could walk freely in the countryside when the wheat was at its golden best, the corn cobs were growing ever taller, rape oil crops were in full bloom and wildflowers were taking their turn to flourish. My favourite wildflowers are poppies. I love how their delicate red petals disperse themselves through the land complementing the yellows and greens of the crops. And having Zig to enjoy these walks with me and him behaving so well added to my pleasure.

The summer before Zig arrived, I used to have a wild rabbit visit my garden. The children next door named him Silky. I delighted in watching Silky from my kitchen window as he pulled away at the branches of one of my rose bushes and munched away at its petals. The thorns were no deterrent to his enjoyment. Maybe I should have been annoyed but I never was, and it was well worth keeping my distance as he fed because he made an excellent job of pruning. Now I had a dog who would dearly love to see the end of this rabbit. I worried when he not only came back but brought a friend with him too. Thankfully, there was never any problem because as soon as I opened the back door, they would quickly run away under the hedges, so rabbits and dog were both able to enjoy the garden.

Dog show...

We had been together for less than a year and it was dog show time. There was a nice one being held just outside the village. Though I knew I had a dog overloaded with energy who I would always have to be careful with, I decided to check out the area. If it was free of livestock in the surrounding area, I would take him to the event to see how he got on. I was not expecting much but the unexpected diversion to our day would make us happy.

We arrived to see a sizeable field with a dog agility area cordoned off to the left. To the right were hot and cold drinks, burgers and hotdogs for sale. There was plenty of space for picnics, and a stall selling dog cake and doggy treats and goods. In the middle was an area cordoned off for the judging.

Once I had got Zig secured to his lead and let him out of the car, he was ready to go. Boy, was he ready to go! He pulled and pulled in excitement and all the time his tail was wagging and he had the biggest doggy grin ever. He thought all his birthdays had come along at once. He knew he was going to have fun. But not before he had calmed down and walked at least somewhat sensibly on his lead. There was a battle of wills and great determination between us, which I won. He was much more settled ten minutes later.

There was so much fun to be had by meeting and socialising with new people and new dog friends, and the weather was beautiful too. Though he was more settled by now and wasn't being any problem, I couldn't help but watch other owners with their dogs who were behaving so well. They were all so expert and relaxed in dog handling, while my skills were so basic. I had to remind myself I was still relatively new to this. I was happy he got no negative attention because he was behaving so well.

While waiting for the judging to begin, he had his first go on an agility circuit. Although he did not know what was expected of him, he was up for the challenge and was willingly coaxed over jumps and ramps. He was a little unsure of the tunnels at first but obliged after a little coaxing. Once he had completed his first circuit and enjoyed a tasty treat at the end, he was keen to go again. He did so well that the circuit supervisor complimented him. He did more circuits and enjoyed every moment. He must be a natural.

After all that activity for us both, it was time to wander around the stalls and purchase an item or two. I bought some homemade dog biscuits and asked about the dog cake. It was homemade and full of healthy and delicious ingredients and looked nice enough in its complete state, but once it was cut into it could have been mistaken for sewage. The dogs would love it. I followed our visits to the stalls by visiting the burger van where I ordered myself a burger and a coffee. I seldom eat meat, but I do find something quite compulsive about buying burgers from a van at a fair or fete. The food was as tasty as expected and the coffee was pure nectar.

Eventually, it was time for the judging. There were ten classes, one of which was a biscuit catching competition, which Zig was useless at, although he did benefit from one treat which he retrieved from the ground. When it came to the dog with the waggiest tail competition, he suddenly got seriously interested in the judges and started sniffing around their ankles as they were about to start the judging. He then decided to sit down. Maybe he had already tired his tail out from all the wagging it had done earlier. I decided to take him out of the arena and sit this one out before the judges got as far as us.

His first success of the day was coming fourth in the most handsome dog competition. As the judges walked along the line-up making their decisions, the youngest of them kept saying, "The brown one, the brown one." I wished they would listen to her and take a good look at him. They were taking a good look at all the dogs and knew what they were doing, but my focus was on Zig. When their decisions were made, he was called out to join the winning four, of which he came fourth. I believe he was robbed, but he was delighted by all the attention and the smell of dog treats coming from the bag of goodies I was given for him.

Toward the end of the afternoon, the judging for best rescue dog was held. I gave a good and honest narrative about where he had come from, what he had been through before adoption and how far we had come together. He sat and waited beside me surprisingly well as I told our story. Once it was done and attention was no longer on him, he pulled on his lead and cried to get back to the agility circuit again. I could not let this happen before the judges' decisions were made. I took him to the far end of the line where it was further away from his vision. When the judges reached us again, one of the younger judges thought he was a lookalike. That caused a little chuckle.

With the judges' decisions made final, Zig and I were asked to come forward first to begin the line-up of the top four winners. I thought we were being called out in reverse order, but no, we had won! Me and my dog who were learning and had so much more to learn together, we had WON.

All the wrong he had done and all the mistakes I had made, were forgotten in that moment. Naturally, that earned him more runs around the agility circuit to tire himself out, and a generous portion of doggy cake when we got home. We had the best of times that afternoon and plenty of goody bags and rosettes to take away with us. When I got home, I went to visit my friend to tell her what a champion dog I had.

Exercising...

When the weather is good, I like to take Zig for a swim. If he is not playing in mud, he is at his happiest in the water. He is a strong swimmer and loves to jump into any bed of water available. Sometimes I take him to Cod Beck, on the River Swale in Thirsk. Here he can enjoy a good play in the sizeable park and jump into the river at any moment he chooses. Before I could let him have his fun I had to teach him not try to chase the ducks as they settled on the river bank or swam near the picnic area. He was soon very good at walking by them on his lead, but I know it's a challenge for him not to follow his instincts. Once passed them and off the lead, he jumps straight in to enjoy his swim.

He was swimming just far enough away from the weir one day when he spied a long and heavy tree bough. He found a good place from which to pull it in his mouth and as he swam, his mighty jaws dragged it from one side of the stream to the other. I was entranced watching him do this and had not realised he had an audience standing on the other side of the river bank who cheered and clapped him when he reached the other side with it. He loves carrying branches, the bigger the better, and if properly trained, he could be a useful stand-in for an elephant wanting a day off.

It is always interesting watching him work on his spatial awareness as he tries to negotiate how to get himself and a large object through a gap too narrow to accommodate him. One day he was trying to get across a bridge with a particularly large piece of forestry held in his mouth. Watching him working out how to do it before walking himself and it across was both amazing and fun as he sidestepped it to the other side

As strong and persistent as he is with these heavy weights, he is a litterbug and does not consider where he leaves these spent items. It is left to me to drag them to a suitable spot where they can be left safely and tidily out of people's way. I never like it when people leave their dog's bulky finds to litter parks or roadways, especially if there is a danger a person can fall over them, perhaps after dark.

After all the effort of having such a strenuous playtime, it was only right that he should join me in enjoying some fish shop fish followed by an ice cream before we went home. This earned him plenty of smiles and attention from passers-by, especially when he was eating the ice cream. Once we finished our little feast, I took him for a walk around the marketplace, so we could digest our food before heading home. The comments I heard about how handsome and what a lovely colour he is further brightened my day. When I was about to get him into the car boot, I noticed a couple looking at him before they approached me and asked if they could say 'Hello'. Well of course they could. I am always happy to talk to anyone about Zig. It helps me get over the times he has been a naughty dog. Boy did they enthuse!

"What a lovely dog he is."

"He is so handsome."

"What a beautiful colour."

"How old is he? How long have you had him? Where did you get him from? Isn't he well behaved?"

The questions went on and on. I enjoyed answering every one of them and telling them about his unfortunate early history and how far we had come together. They told me I had done well with him and how lucky I am to have him and wished he was their dog. This was an especially memorable conversation, but wherever we go (well mostly), I am told what a handsome, well behaved and lovely dog he is. I do not forget our slip-ups, and sometimes admit to him having his negative moments, but I never disagree with the positive comments. It always reminds me how far we have come and what a terror he was when I first got him.

Part Three: Difficult Times

In the December, I was fortunate enough to be invited to Peru to spend the holidays with my son David and his partner Karina. We had a lovely Christmas and New Year together, all at my Son's expense, discovering Lima and meeting my future daughter-in-law's family and their friends.

This was the first time I had left Zig in kennels for any longer than an overnight stay, and I would always be desperate to have him back even after just that short time. Leaving him and being without him for three weeks was going to be purgatory for me.

On the evening I left him at the kennels, I was shown his run. It was spacious and dry with comfortable bedding and it was well heated. I left him with a few new toys and a blanket for comfort. I doubted any of these would be intact when I returned. Buying toys for Zig is a waste of time and money as he has them chewed up and spat out in no time. However, I felt better leaving them for him. The kennel staff already had contact details for the vets, so I knew all his needs would be catered for. I tried to reassure myself but could not get out of my mind the thought that he might be seriously injured, or even die while I was away. There was no logical reason why he should die or get hurt but I still worried.

Because he is such a sociable dog and knows the kennel staff, he was happy to watch me go. Even so, I worried he would be fretting after me and that the staff may not be able to cope with him for such a long time. Even more concerning for me was that he might revert to his old behaviours.

I need not have worried because he didn't. To help me enjoy my holiday and ease my concerns I was sent daily photographs and videos via Facebook of him playing with other canine boarders. This helped tremendously. Even so, I missed him more than I can say.

On my return to England in early January, I went to collect him as soon as I could. When he saw me, he jumped off the salon worktop he had been placed on to have his fur dried after his bath. His cries of delight were audible for all to hear, his front paws clung to my shoulders as he licked my neck, his tail wagging so vigorously, he could have done a rough dry of the other dogs after their baths. Unfortunately, he relieved himself on the floor too. I was dismayed about this, but the staff told me that this sometimes happens when a dog is so excited.

Bringing him back home was such a delight and relief for me. It was so nice to have him with me again, but I knew I would never have any more worries booking him into those kennels again. Now whenever he sees any of the staff, his delight is proof of how much he loves them.

A tough year ahead...

2014 was to prove my most trying year in keeping us together. By now I felt we had come as far as we could with his training and I knew his boundaries. But there were to be some memorable events ahead of us and not all fortunate.

My son, David, had come home for a few weeks in the January and it was lovely to have his company when he had time out of his busy schedule. He came with us on our walks whenever he could. I took advantage of his stronger muscles when Zig was on the lead, especially as I had decided it would be a good time to try walking him near sheep again. He was not well behaved (Zig that is). He showed no restraint in his drive to get to them; the surrounding field fences would have been no barrier had he been off the lead. Until David had to leave, he would take Zig from me and control him as we passed the field. His time with us was of great value in Zig's learning to be better behaved when near livestock.

Before David went home, we took Zig for a swim in a river about a thirty-minute drive away. We intended to walk about two miles along the river banks while Zig ran up and down, dipping in an out of the water as he pleased. Knowing he was a safe and strong swimmer we carried on with our walk while Zig played. Suddenly, we heard what we thought to be the desperate cries of a dog struggling and in danger. David turned on his heels and ran towards Zig in his endeavour to rescue him from whatever was causing his distress. When we saw him, the vision before us was not one of a dog in peril but of one trying to dislodge a tree by its roots at the water's edge. All the noise he was making was simply because he could not get his toy out of the box, so to speak. Getting him to leave the tree and come with us was easy enough, but it left us calf-deep in mud. We had also misjudged our time out and had a little difficulty finding our way back to the car in the rapidly darkening evening sky. There would also be a car to clean tomorrow.

When David and I Skyped each other after his return home, I was delighted to be able to report continued improvement in Zig's behaviour and to tell him how easy it now was to walk him near sheep. Though I would never dream of walking him through a field of sheep, there was no problem in walking him by one.

In May, just two days after my 60th birthday, we had just started our afternoon walk when suddenly my feet slipped on the shingle underneath me. Before I knew it I had hit the ground. The first thing that worried me was the possibility of spinal injury. I had had a lower disc removed in the late eighties and thankfully the operation was a great success, but I am always wary of injuring it again. Fortunately, all was well there, but unfortunately, I could not weight bear on my right foot.

The ground was dry, the day was warm and bright, and Zig's behaviour was exemplary. He hadn't been pulling on his lead and I had been feeling rather smug about this. It just goes to show pride really does come before a fall. After the event, he stood and waited patiently by my side until help arrived. However, he showed no concern for my well-being.

As is often the case, the times when you need to take friends up on offers of help are the times when they are unavailable to help you. On that day, all my local friends were away from their homes for one reason or another.

I sat in the lane having tried and failed to stand and walk and waiting and hoping for help to arrive. A man who had been working on some overhead cables was standing some distance behind us as he spoke to me.

"Are yee alreet Mrs?"

"I don't think so. I can't stand up."

"Ere Mrs, I'm petrified of yer dog."

"No need to worry he is very safe to be with." Zig was still waiting very patiently by my side, but this man was too afraid to come any closer. Thankfully, he was not going to leave me until he had me safely attended to.

"Can I go and get ye some help from anywhere?"

Who on earth was I going to call on? Every friend I knew in the village was away for a few days, and I did not want to call on acquaintances.

The only person I could think to ask him to call on was my neighbour, Carol, and I was concerned about asking him to call on her as her health is not too good. I could think of no one else, but I was worried she would not be able to cope with such a situation.

Once he had gone to get her, I realised it was coming close to the time when the primary school children were to be collected by their parents. As I sat on the grass waiting, the only people to pass me by on foot were a man and a young boy. The man stopped and asked if I was alright. I told him I had injured my foot and help was on its way. He said he had to go and collect his other child from school and would check on me if I was still there when he got back. I never saw him again, so I guess I had been taken home by the time he got back up the hill with his children.

The workman returned to let me know assistance would be with us shortly and waited at his comfortable distance until she arrived.

Carol could not have been more helpful. She arrived in her brand-new car which she parked as close to us as she could.

"I'll get Zig in the back for you first," she said.

I thought it might have been better for her to take him home on foot first to ensure the cleanliness of her car, and to come back for me. I would have been alright for the extra five minutes it would take her.

"But he'll have hair all over your new car," I protested.

"That's okay," she said, making it obvious I did not need to worry.

The man waited until Zig was in the car before helping to get me safely seated in the back where I could put my foot up.

Before he left us, he let us know he was a part-time sports physiotherapist and advised me to keep my foot elevated and get to A&E before too long.

I often think about this unexpected saviour, who had never met me before. He was so afraid of my dog but was determined to do all he could to get me assistance. I will never be able to thank him enough.

Being driven the short distance home, I was more concerned by the dog hair being shed and laid down by Zig than I was about my foot. Having got Zig out of her car and into the house, Carol helped me to the sofa before going to the kitchen to put the kettle on. Meanwhile, she wrote a shopping list of what I would need for the next few days. Coffee made, she went shopping and came back not only with essentials but with a veritable banquet which she put in the cupboards and fridge for me.

"My purse is in my bag; how much do I owe you?"

"Nothing Kathy, this is what friends and neighbours do for each other."

I knew I would be chastised if I laboured the point, so I thanked her for her generosity.

Before she left me, she gave strict instructions for me to call her again if I needed anything else. What a star she was; I will be forever grateful.

Poor Zig did not get his walk that afternoon. He too was being a star in his own way.

I called on Wendy, who I knew had a few days off work. Though not local to me she is very willing and reliable, and at the time, the nearest person I could call on to come and stay with me. She was more than happy to do this providing it would be okay with her husband, which it was.

When she arrived, she took one look at my foot and said, "That looks broken Kathy."

"No, it won't be broken, it's just badly sprained. It doesn't hurt while I'm just sat here." Although happy to elevate my leg as advised, I was in no hurry to go to A&E.

"Well I think it's broken," she insisted.

"Don't be daft; it doesn't hurt until I try to walk on it. If it was broken it would be hurting all the time," I insisted further.

Being a less dominant person than most people, she said no more and went to the kitchen to make a hot drink for both of us.

I had to get Zig kennelled for a few days until I was back on my feet, so I called on the boarding kennels staff I knew so well by now. As willing as Wendy would be to walk him, she is a very slight person and I could not trust that she would be able to control Zig.

After explaining my plight to the manager and owner, she was at my door ready to collect him in 10 minutes. She came in to talk to me while Wendy got the lead from the kitchen.

As she was attaching the lead to Zig's collar, she looked at my foot and said, "That looks awful Kathy, it makes me sick to look at it." She did look pale. She was very busy and had to refuse the cup of tea offered. After chatting for a few more minutes making sure she looked at my face and not my foot, a very busy kennel owner and manager took him away to stay with her for a few days. Little did any of us know how long these few days were going to last.

Once she had gone, Wendy made a meal for us. As she was cooking, I took the time to have a good look at my foot and wondered if I had dislocated it, but I persuaded myself I had not. Still no need to go to A&E, I reckoned. I said nothing to Wendy. The meal was delicious.

Being the stubborn, tenacious and determined character I am, I decided to follow Wendy, who was doing a light dusting and vacuuming upstairs in readiness for my son and partner's arrival the next day.

Despite her protestations, I insisted I could be of some

help, provided I did not put any weight on the affected ankle.

Satisfied I had done what I could, I made my way downstairs on my bottom. Having reached the last step, I stood up and hopped the short distance towards the living room and sofa. I was almost there when I fell over and felt tremendous pain as I repositioned my dislocated ankle. Yes, I did make a lot of noise about it and was still trying to control my breathing through the pain when Wendy arrived by my side; "Did that hurt?"

"You bet it did," I said through gritted teeth.

Having sat back on the sofa with my leg elevated, I re-examined my foot. Although still swollen, it was in a much better position; confirmation I had dislocated it in the earlier fall. I thought it would start to get better now. I slept on the sofa that night.

The next morning Wendy, who had stayed overnight, was as ready as ever to help.

Alice and her husband Tom arrived home to an answer-phone message from me briefly letting them know what I had done. I soon had a visit from her, so I could give a full account of what had happened. She took me at my word when I told her I had dislocated my ankle and relocated it when I fell again in the living room. She let me know she was happy to take me to A&E if needs be. None of us realised just how soon I would be taking her up on her offer.

After she left us, I finally decided I would phone my GP's surgery just to confirm I did not need to go to A&E. Turns out, I did. I allowed what I thought would be sufficient time for Alice to have a meal with her family before calling on her to ask if I could claim the favour she'd offered of driving me to the hospital.

On the way, Wendy and I batted opinions back and forth as to whether I had a break or not.

It was decided that if I did have a break, we were not going to allow Wendy into the car on the way home. Such smugness could not have been tolerated.

I was helped into a wheelchair and taken to the A&E department where I waited in a queue to see a doctor. There were plenty of people to be seen before me. Wendy, ever the mother hen, bought us all a much-appreciated hot drink.

When called to the next available cubicle, I was asked to transfer from wheelchair to chair and wait to be seen by a doctor. As I was transferring, the nurse realised I couldn't weight bear on the foot. "Stay where you are," she said.

She examined my lower leg and I was sent for an x-ray straight away. Wheeled to the department by Wendy we were given the resulting films by the radiographer to be taken to the sister.

The x-rays confirmed I had multiple fractures to my ankle.

The A&E sister put the films on the lightbox and explained to us all what I had done. Both friends were nodding sagely as she showed us where the fractures were. I was doing the same from my wheelchair, wondering what the hell she was talking about. If it was anyone else's x-rays I was being shown, I am sure I would have understood them no problem. I had seen enough before to know what they were all about. But I was finding it harder to do so when it was about me and I could not take a step back from the situation (no pun intended). Once explanations had been given, she told me she was making arrangements to take me to the ward to await surgery.

What! No plaster of Paris before being sent home?

"No, I can't go to the ward tonight, I will have to come back tomorrow, my son and his partner will be arriving from Peru tonight. I have to be home to let them in," I protested.

"Someone will have to help out," she said. "You're going to the ward."

Alice took care of this. Meanwhile, I waited in a hospital bed for the safe arrival of David and Karina.

They were to spend too much of their precious time in the UK visiting me in hospital.

I was given a talking to by the nursing and surgical staff for having waited so long before going to A&E. The delay meant I would not be operated on for a few more days until the skin around my ankle had settled down.

The surgery and post-operative physiotherapy went well, but I was to be unable to weight bear for at least six weeks.

Meanwhile, Zig stayed in kennels.

Financial strain...

Because of pain in my arms, I was unable to make much use of the crutches provided so I borrowed Alice's mother's old walker which had a seat with it. This meant I was able to push myself backwards in it using my good foot. A high stool was provided for me by therapy staff from the hospital to help me wash at the sink and prepare simple meals, but I kept slipping out of it. Trying to do without it meant I was struggling with my balance. Alice pulled the kitchen table over to the sink, so I was able to perch on the side of it. This worked out much better.

If I needed to go out shopping, Alice would drive me to the supermarket and push me in a wheelchair and get any products I could not reach from the higher shelves before driving me back home, putting my shopping away and helping me settle in again.

She or her husband made my evening meals and she would bring them plated up and on a tray each evening. Later, she would walk down the hill from her house to collect her crockery. Claire, a friend from the other end of the village, brought lunch to me each day and kept me company for a while. More amazing good friends who were there when I needed them.

I needed all this help and could not have taken Zig out for any of his walks, which would have been detrimental to his physical and mental health.

On this occasion, the insurance company let me down. I had not worried at all about the cost of kennels because I have top notch insurance for Zig. But when the time came for me to put my claim in, I was told insurance would only be paid out for kennelling if I was in hospital for longer than five days and only until the day I was discharged.

This was one of those occasions when you learn you have true friends where sometimes you least expect them. When Beth came to visit me after a day's work, she said to me, "I'll pay Zig's kennel fees for you." I could hardly believe what I was hearing, and my heart skipped a beat in gratitude at this lovely, genuine offer. I thanked her but did not accept as I knew it would be too great an expense. When I told her months later how much the bill came to, I think she must have been relieved I had refused her offer, though she did say she would have paid it, and I believe she would. She was beating the insurance company hands down and it wasn't her I was paying my fees to.

Once Alice realised Zig would have to be kennelled for so long and what a costly expense it would be, she telephoned the RSPCA to ask them if they could take care of him or knew of anybody who could foster him while I was incapacitated. She was very careful to ensure they knew what a loved dog he was, so they would know not to be concerned about his welfare. Unfortunately, they could not offer any help. I had not thought to contact them and was very appreciative to know what she had done. However, I did think to contact national and local charity dog walkers to ask if they could help. To be eligible for help from these charities I needed to be over 60 years of age. Having celebrated this milestone hardly more than a week earlier, I fitted their criteria. Unfortunately, they were unable to be of assistance as they either had no dog walkers in my area or could not cope with a dog the size of Zig.

It was three months plus before I could walk sufficiently well to have Zig home.

Kennels are a costly necessity at times and bills must be paid. Having only a small pension to live on made me worry about how I would manage, but the kennel owner was very generous with me. Plus, when she brought Zig home, she was armed with food and a doggy toy and chew hamper because he had been with her for so long. I thought that such a nice thing to do.

More bad luck...

I'd had Zig for over two years now and if there was no livestock about, I went back to practising his recall training which he had to relearn after his long spell in kennels. I was pleased with how quickly he picked it up again. He was stopping and waiting for me on command and would come to me when called. He even remembered to wait for me at certain places until I reattached his lead.

Not too many weeks after having got over my trauma, we were walking towards a rural coffee shop which was a halfway stop on one of our walks. He stopped, as usual, behind a farm gate and was waiting for me when he heard a tractor and trailer coming up the road.

I could see him weighing up the situation as I gave him the 'Wait' command, his head turning to me as I called, before turning back towards the noise from the road. I knew I was losing this fight.

Despite all our hard work together and him doing so well, my command was useless. His excitement was too highly piqued for him to resist as the vehicle came closer. He charged past the side post of the closed gate through a gap in the hedge and chased after the moving machinery. I knew he would come out the loser, and he did.

I heard the impact and a pathetic yelp. The feeble and sorry sight that walked towards me was nauseating. I could not understand how he had not been killed and was managing to walk back to me after what had just happened. The tractor and trailer carried on with its journey. I checked the wound. It was long and deep. Amazingly there was little obvious blood loss but the deep cut was gaping.

We were on an empty country lane with not another soul in sight and me not knowing what to do for the best. I was unable to pick him up and carry him; he was far too heavy. I was worried about leaving him alone and frightened while I walked to the road to stop a passing driver. If I did that maybe a well-intentioned person would come back to help and be frightened off by the sight of his wound. The nearest source of help was the coffee shop, but that was a good three minutes away from where we were and was going to take longer with Zig as traumatised as he was. What was I to do?

As reluctant as I was about it, I knew I had no option but to walk him there. If a motorist was passing by, I would try and flag them down, but not one car passed us. I worried with every step we took that he would collapse from shock and exhaustion. I will never know how he walked the distance with such an injury.

The cafe owner and staff were always friendly, and best of all they allowed dogs into their premises. This was of particular help to me in the early days when I was teaching Zig to sit and wait patiently. At first, he would be very active all the time we were there, but he soon learned to sit quietly and wait while I had my coffee. He had also become a good 'pat dog' which earned him plenty of attention from admiring customers, adults and children who would have many questions to ask me about his mix of breed and background history. Whatever I told them about his breed mixes I was always told how handsome he was. Some children drew pictures of him and would proudly show me the results of their fine artwork. The only damage he ever did in the shop was accidental when he knocked a piece of pottery off a shelf with his tail as we were walking in. That was a very expensive visit.

We walked to the cafe's kitchen window where I explained to the gentleman what had happened and asked if I could use his landline to make an emergency phone call to the vets. Mobile phone reception is barely existent in this area. If it had been better, I could have called the vets from where we were when the injury took place. Once the call was made the gentleman's partner, owner and business curator came out with a chair for me to rest on while we waited for the vet to arrive. I was also treated to a most welcome cup of coffee.

The lady was unsure about how to handle this situation. "I can't look," she said half turning away while tentatively looking through parted middle fingers at what she did not want to see.

The vet arrived, and, after a quick assessment, Zig was walked the short way to the car. On our way to the surgery, I was given a rundown of the possible extent of his injuries. Shock being the biggest concern. My impressions of the severity of the injuries were greater than his at the time.

I needed to be dropped off at my house, before the vet continued the journey to the surgery, while I quickly grabbed my purse and car keys before following them in my car. I arrived not many minutes after them and Zig was already waiting comfortably in a cage having been started on intravenous fluids to help raise his blood pressure and treat him for shock before they anaesthetised him. I was allowed in to see him and gave him as much comfort and reassurance as I could. I hoped he was benefiting from this as much as I was. There was nothing more I could do now but drive back home and wait for news.

I was not home for long before I received a phone call from the vet while Zig was in surgery. He explained that the injuries Zig had sustained were far more serious than had at first been thought. There was a large scuffed and deep penetrating wound from his neck to his chest, and because of deeper previously unseen injuries around the wound, the prognosis was poor. If he was to survive the operation, nerve damage to certain areas could cause problems with his walking and worse still, could result in his being unable to swallow. In short, his injuries could prove fatal.

I was unsurprised to learn that the injuries were worse than was first thought. But their extent and his possible prognosis was devastating news. As painful as it would be for me, I was unwilling to watch him waste away from not being able to swallow properly. But having faith and knowing he was in no distress while anaesthetised, I decided to let him go through the operation. I crossed my fingers and hoped for the best.

Thanks to the care and skills of these wonderful people, he did pull through. His injuries were repaired and his wound extended in order to form a decent surgical closure of the torn skin and muscles. Phew, he had made it! He remained on intravenous fluids and antibiotics to fight off infection.

On the day he was to come home, the vet who had initially taken Zig to the surgery and assisted in his operation, helped me settle him into the boot of my car. On the way out he was telling me what a lovely dog I had. (Smiles of pride and gratitude from me.) "You have a lovely dog. A very lucky dog, but a lovely dog," he said.

The evening after taking him home I felt it necessary to contact the on-call vet and explain that there was a fist-sized blood-filled swelling along the suture line of Zig's chest. I was able to report that he was bright and alert and not showing any signs of pain or problems with his breathing. I was reassured and then advised to visit the surgery in the morning if it was no better. When I woke, I was expecting to find I had to do exactly as advised but the swelling had completely disappeared. As he was licking and scratching where he could reach on the wound, I was advised to put a t-shirt on him and tie it at the bottom to deter him from doing so. He looked like Top Cat's canine alter ego, all dressed up on his top half and wearing not a stitch on the bottom. But it did work well.

Less than two weeks after his near-fatal injury, his stitches were taken out and he was free to exercise as tolerated.

Fortunately, no worrying complications occurred. I followed the post-operative instructions to the letter and he made such a good recovery. You would never know he had had such a serious injury. Needless to say the costs of all his treatment was plentiful. Thank goodness for insurance because on this occasion, they did pay out.

Thankfully, he has never chased traffic again and is perfectly well behaved when near it.

Operations well and truly behind us both, we were enjoying our walks; the weather was beautiful and appropriate for the season. Being able to drive again, I would take him further afield for a good swim, which he loves to do, or let him run through park and woodland hedges and shrubbery. Often, he would reappear from behind a hedge or some scrub, covered in goosegrass, thistle flowers, sticky jacks and looking fully garnished and ready for the oven. These things can be difficult to get rid of, but I was so happy about our lives returning to normal that I would see the funny side. We would both relax while I rid him of any forestry he had stuck to him before going on our way.

Now we only had to get through Winter safely. That would not be an easy achievement as I was now faced with more of his pulling.

The one-off payment I had received from my pension when I left work in 2012 had dwindled to nothing and I was living on my small monthly payments. However, I was concerned he might cause me to fall on the ice, so I asked the dog trainer to do a few more sessions with me before the season changed. I went through all I was told to do and practised better lead behaviour with him when I could, but once again I failed. No falls or broken bones though. Hallelujah!

We were in our third year together now and I was letting him off the lead in a car-free area of the village. For a long time now, I had had no problem with his recall or keeping him away from the road. We were meeting other walkers and their dogs, and humans and canines alike were pleased to meet each other.

Sometimes just walking in the park was the best place for meetups. I remember one day meeting with a lady I had gotten to know quite well. She was a well-spoken woman whose company I enjoyed. We were in idle conversation when her dog cocked its leg up and weed down my lower leg and on to my boot. The poor woman's embarrassment held no bounds and she could not stop apologising to me. "It really is alright, it will all come out in the wash," I said to her. I was surprised at her when still red-faced, she bent down to her dog, gently cupped its muzzle in her hand and with the gentlest and most refined voice said; "Dog, you bastard." Not the worst word to hear coming out of someone's mouth, but from her, it sounded so funny.

Health issues...

As difficult as 2014 was, 2015 was not going to treat me any kinder. After enjoying some good times off from my annoying health issues, I became poorly again and was finding it difficult to look after myself. I could not get up the stairs to go to bed each night. Fortunately, I have a downstairs toilet and a narrow hallway so I could stretch my hands out to the walls on each side for support if necessary while I walked there. I had to force myself up the stairs once a week for a bath, I could not manage any more, and was so fatigued and out of breath by the time I got to the top of the stairs, I had to go and lie on my bed and often would fall asleep. On those nights, I would sleep in my bed.

Friends were very good at helping me out where they could, and Detta and Maria came to help me for a few weeks. As much as I was struggling, I still had a very active dog to walk. Just letting him out to the garden to do his toileting and have a sniff around was enough of an effort. I did not have the finances to afford a dog walker, so I had no choice but to do his walks. I was still able to drive but was finding it difficult to do so. I would take us to the park a couple of miles away because there was some seating scattered around and the land was flatter there. Maria would join me for these walks and I found her presence very reassuring.

I contacted national and local dog walking charities again asking for help but had no luck this time either for the same reasons as when I had broken my ankle.

A dread overcame me at the thought that I might have to let him go to a new home because I was finding it so difficult to cope financially and physically.

Because of his mix of breed and initial unsociable behaviours, I worried that he might be taken by someone who would want to use him for fighting. The thought that he might be used for such a thing would have my soul almost crushed. No, I could not do that. I would just have to work through my breathing, pain and mobility problems and take him out for his exercise.

Getting through those times was more difficult than I could even begin to describe. I guess I am made of extra tough stuff because I did get through it. Soon after, I had to give up my car because I was having trouble concentrating and understanding the sequence of the traffic lights and road signs. My hands and arms would pain from steering the wheel, and my legs were refusing to cooperate when I got out of the vehicle after even a short journey. Plus, it was not financially viable for me anymore. Having to do without this commodity meant walks were restricted to the village and close surrounding areas.

As we all know, walking the same route every day can become tiresome to the spirit, so I thought I should try taking Zig on a bus. He did not like his first journey at all and pressed his body to my knees for security all the way, even though it was only a five-minute journey. It did not stop him enjoying his play in the park and he was a little less unsure on our journey home. A few trips later he knew that getting on the bus was going to lead to fun. He was then so keen to get on he would try and bypass other passengers before they had time to move. They would be happy to let him on first, but I told them he must wait and show some manners.

I have talked of my health struggles while keeping Zig not because I feel the need to share my sometimes-frail health with you, but because as informative, and hopefully compelling, Zig's history is, it is not sufficient to complete this book on its own. (Sorry, poor attempts at humour over). Throughout my health and financial difficulties, keeping and providing for him has, at times, been a great challenge. But on adopting him, I took full responsibility for him so must be prepared for times like this. However, all these difficulties pale into insignificance once they are over and the love and care I give is repaid in dividends. If you want a loyal pet, get yourself a dog.

A welcome break...

Carol, who helped me out by taking me home in her car when I had broken my ankle, has a house on the northeast coast and she offered me and a couple of friends the chance to spend a long weekend there free of charge. I was even able to take Zig. Unfortunately, Wendy was not able to join us. However, Claire was delighted to be asked and was happy to do the driving and for Zig to ride in the back of her car. Plans were made, and the day came to pack up the car with humans and dog and all things necessary for our time away. Off we went. When we arrived, we found the accommodation was lovely and knew we were going to enjoy our time there.

Once we had unpacked and enjoyed a light snack, we prepared for what was to be a leisurely stroll through town. Aargh! I had forgotten to pack Zig's noseband and with all the new places and smells to discover, not to mention all the places to cock his leg up and wee, he was pulling on his lead like an ox on steroids. I needed to find a pet supply store as quickly as possible, but the only one was at the far end of town from where we were staying. I did not see much of my surroundings on the way there as it was all a blur of struggling to stay upright and avoid crashing into people. When we arrived, both Claire and I were exhausted. Not Zig though, he had plenty more energy to carry on exploring.

In the shop, I asked the assistant for the type of noseband I wanted and was relieved to learn they had them in stock. The shop owner, having followed us in, heard what I was asking for and interrupted the purchase, telling me he had been watching me trying to control my dog and the noseband

I was asking for was not enough to control a dog like him. It had worked well enough before, but I listened to what he had to say as he took a figure of eight rope lead from his stock and with my permission showed me how to fit it around Zig's neck and muzzle. Then he walked outside with Zig and me and instructed me on how to hold the lead to get the best control. It worked wonderfully well, and I was able to relax walking my dog. Having done a small circuit of the area, we returned to the shop and I bought two new leads. As we were walking with a much easier to control dog, Claire said she could not believe what a difference there now was in his walking. We had a leisurely walk along the pier stopping to have a light lunch before going home.

As with all nosebands I tried, he quickly learnt how to work past the control it was supposed to provide. When he wasn't working out how to get it off with his paws, he was scraping his face along the grass to give himself a good scratch because it irritated him. Looking at him wearing it once we were home again, I thought the depth of the rope might be partially blocking his vision. So, I went back to using the one he was used to. He still scrapes his nose along the grass, but he can see much better and cannot get this one off. *'Two figure-of eight dog leads free to a good home. Dog not included'.*

The weather on the coast was cool and drizzly for the next few days. As we strolled along the beach, Zig enjoyed running on the sand and splashing about at the edge of the ocean. He tasted a little of the salty sea water but was wary at the depths and expanse of this particular body of water. He did not go as far in as he normally would when he got the chance of a good swim.

After enjoying one of our walks and having a good afternoon, we stopped for a coffee and a snack at one of the beachside cafes. The effects of Zig having drunk the salt water became all too apparent as he vomited on the veranda. What an embarrassment! The staff were very good about it but equally pleased when I offered to clean it up before we went on our way. We were sat outside in a place hidden from the other customers, so they had not known what had happened. He was given some clean, fresh water before we left. We took another little walk to make sure his stomach had settled before getting into the car. More shame. As if to spite our caution, he was sick again in the back of Claire's car. 'Oh no! not in her new car!' Claire is an unflustered kind of person and was as patient and understanding as ever over this. I was mortified. As soon as we got back to our accommodation, I made sure I thoroughly cleaned the soiled seat. It was a liquid only diet for him that night.

I took him out for his evening walk while Claire prepared a meal for us. I did very well not getting us too lost finding my way to the local park. However, I failed miserably trying to get us back to the house and had us walking an extra mile before I knew where I was again. Luckily it was salad for tea.

Some dogs we met were friendly and always ready to play. Others were timid or snappy. Dogs have different temperaments and personalities just as we do, and this should be understood. Owners should be aware of the size and fitness of their dogs too. I watched two dog owners drag their dogs up some concrete steps; it was distressing. Thankfully, there weren't so many steps that the dogs would be physically hurt, but they were short of breath on getting to the top. The pulling at their neck could not have been good for them. I could only worry about the traumas these poor little beings were going through. Being in a seaside town and not knowing any animal protection organisations I could visit I felt there was little I could do. Thankfully, once they reached the top of the steps, they found it a little easier to keep up with their walkers. Why don't these people think about what they are doing?

Having returned home after our lovely weekend, it was back to normal for Zig and me. Walking around the village felt good again for a while, but we were soon ready to get back on a bus so we could meet friends and play in the park. He was still only used to making short journeys and I wondered how he would cope if we went further afield. I was worried about him having a wee on public transport before we reached our destination. I reasoned he would be okay, but it took me some time to convince myself we should try. It was the hot weather that had me decide to go for it. I felt for him in the heat as he panted throughout the day and night to cool himself off. He needed to get to a stream to cool his overall temperature. The half-hour of bliss would keep him cooler for a good time afterwards.

More visits to the vet...

Another autumn came and went and once again I was enjoying the changes in the land around me. The trees were dropping conkers ready for young boys and girls to collect. Pine trees were beginning to drop cones of various sizes; I wondered about taking some home to spray gold or silver for the Christmas season but decided I had enough. People were wearing warmer weatherproof clothing again. It was back to covering the floors at home to protect them from muddy feet and going through the actions of dog cleaning again before he could come into the house.

In the December, I had cause to take Zig to the vets again because he was off his food and water and was limping on each hind limb in an alternating manner. Clinical examination found no obvious cause for him to be off his food so maybe it was because he was in pain. I was advised to restart him on anti-inflammatory medicine once he started eating again. Because he was eating a little in the mornings, I decided to go ahead and treat his pain, giving him his medicine with his breakfast. Three days later I took him back because he still was not eating or drinking properly, had vomited that morning and was reluctant to go for his walks.

On re-examination, it was noted that his lameness had not improved as would be expected but the vet thought this might be due to his current poorly condition. After some discussion, it was decided to continue with the anti-inflammatories and to keep to a diet of bland food and plenty of water. If that did not work for him, he was to return for blood tests and antibiotic therapy. Improvement was gradual but a return visit for blood tests was not necessary.

In March of 2016, although otherwise healthy, Zig suddenly became lame again. This time in his left front leg. There was nothing I could think of that would have caused this, but he was obviously in pain and unable to walk normally. He was also a long way behind me when we were out, so I kept his walk short. Reluctantly, it was back to the vets again. I had given him a dose of the anti-inflammatory medication left over from his last episode of lameness, which served him well. By the time we got to the vets, he was much happier and walking better. The advice was to continue the usual medication and do lead walks only for the next few days. Once again, the treatment did the trick, but I was concerned that such a young dog was having so many episodes involving painful limbs and lameness. He was hardly four years old and past the age of growing pains. He is as typical as all dogs; once he feels better and forgets he has ever had a problem, he gets back to racing and chasing.

Our next visit, for a change, was not because of lameness. I thought he might have caught a mild dose of kennel cough. Perhaps I was over cautious on this visit, but I did not think it right to take the chance where his health was concerned. I was also considering the possibility he might infect other dogs if my diagnosis was right. He always has his kennel cough vaccine when it is due, but it would seem he had caught a strain the vaccine could not cover on this occasion. He was not too affected by it but had to be kept away from other dogs until the incubation period of ten days had passed. He was still able to walk with me to the coffee shop outside the village and enjoy a swim in the stream on their land and could run freely in the open fields if no other dogs were about.

Zig was my first concern throughout these episodes. I

would never think of ignoring his health issues, especially if he is in pain, but I was feeling despondent about how frequently he needed to visit the surgery. I also had concerns about the money it was costing me, even with his insurance, and hoped it would be a long time before we would have to go back again.

Naughty dog…

When you read of our next episode, please do not think I am not vigilant when in charge of Zig. I had learnt the hard way following the incident with the hens. But, horror of horrors, he let me down in the worst way imaginable.

We were nearing home after our long afternoon walk. He was tired and walking at a nice steady pace beside me while attached to his noseband and lead. Suddenly he pulled away and I was left with only his lead in my hand. Thirty seconds later there was a dead cat on someone's lawn. There were no obvious injuries, and the cat looked completely at peace.

'Why Zig, Why? You have been doing so well,' I was screaming inside. Deed done, he came back to me wagging his tail as though he had done the world a favour. But he hadn't. He had just unnecessarily destroyed a family's much-loved pet.

I reattached his lead to his noseband and looked down at the cat for its identity tag, then as gently and respectfully as I could, picked it up and cradled it in my arms for the rest of our walk home.

Once indoors, I carefully wrapped it in a towel and placed it in a box to make it look as though it was asleep in bed and as peaceful as could be before putting it in the garden shed out of Zig's reach. Then, owning up to my sins again, I picked up the telephone handset and dialled the number on the identity tag. This was a very difficult conversation for both of us. To this day I cannot convey how sorry I am about what he did.

While waiting for the cat to be collected, I examined Zig's noseband and collar to work out how he had managed to pull away, to find I had only attached his lead to his identity tag wire. Another thing to be more alert over, and I always have been since.

Once the cat had been collected, and my heartfelt apologies given once again, I started to worry over what to do about Zig. He had just done the worst thing imaginable in unnecessarily killing this much-loved family pet.

Forgetting about what he had done was impossible; fear was growing inside me that he would have to be put to sleep. I kept looking at him, oblivious to the harm and upset he had caused. Hating him for what he had done and thinking about how he had undone all our good work together. He had been so good for such a long time. I was so very angry with him and really could not find it in my soul to like him very much. However, I still worried about what was to become of him. I had made a promise to myself to keep him through thick and thin and now I was wondering if I was going to be allowed to.

Why did he do it?

Why did I not check I had attached his lead properly?

That night I tossed and turned when in bed and paced the house when I was not. Sleep was not going to happen for me that night, and my sister Maria and her daughter Rachael were coming to stay with me the next afternoon for a couple of days.

Having collected my visitors from the train station, I told them of the sad chain of events of the day before and explained that I would be calling at the RSPCA on our way home.

I left them waiting in the car while I went to speak to a member of staff, dreading the outcome with every step I took.

It was their quiet time, but a lady kindly sat with me and listened while I told her about the traumas of the day before.

"You need to get him a muzzle," she said.

A muzzle! No mention of him being euthanised. Why didn't I think of that, instead of imagining that my young dog's life would soon be at an end? I was expecting to be mourning the loss of my beloved pet, just as the cat's family were mourning theirs.

There were no muzzles to fit him at the centre, so we went to look for one elsewhere on our way home.

We found a good one to fit him which Maria bought, along with some tasty dog treats from a small pet supply store.

I rely on his noseband to keep control of him when out walking and was going to have to work out how to fit the muzzle on him at the same time. The only way to secure them together was to weave the straps of the noseband through the narrow slots of the muzzle. Because of my finer dexterity problems and the pain when doing certain manoeuvres with my hand and fingers, I found this very difficult to do. Adding to this, he was spending even more of his time scraping his nose along the ground or clawing at them trying to remove them from his snout. On top of these difficulties, while wearing the muzzle, he would react badly to other dogs. With the exception of what had happened after being hit by the car two years earlier, this was not his normal behaviour.

As Maria and Rachael had gone to visit York the next day, I went to visit the cat's owner to let her know what steps I had taken to avoid a repeat of such an event. She was very gracious as she invited me into her home and told me how she recognised my honesty. But I thought it only right she and her family knew what I had done after what had happened to their cat, so they could mourn and manage the end of its life knowing I had done all I reasonably could to stop such a thing happening again.

I continued with my struggles to put the muzzle and noseband on together for as long as I could before deciding to abandon the muzzle in favour of the noseband. My reasons for doing this was because the pain, weakness and poor dexterity in my fingers was worsening from threading the noseband straps through the muzzle. Given the choice of having control over his pulling, or keeping the muzzle on him, I chose the noseband as the safer option as he is unable to pull away from me and worry farm animals. This has never failed me. And he is friendlier without the muzzle.

The only other hitch I have had since then was when he was vying for dominance with other dogs. They would always be male dogs who were larger than him. Most owners would say, "Just let them sort themselves out." A few would be unhappy. But whatever their reaction I would always put him back on his lead, apologise and take him away. However, it was not long before he stopped this and now, he ignores them or walks away. He never barges at other dogs and if he gets too close to smaller dogs, he is the one who might get a good telling off and maybe a nip, but he never reciprocates. He tolerates them well and will stand patiently while being investigated, just as other dogs would do for him during the early training of his errant misspent youth. There is no pretending he is not still a live wire, but he knows and respects boundaries.

My brother Andrew and his wife Laura came from Holland to visit. They too are dog lovers and are very physically fit. Having had to leave their dog at home, they were missing the regularity of their walks so were keen to keep Zig and me company when we went out. I was even spoilt with a few lazy mornings when Andrew offered to take him out for morning walks. Zig was spoilt too because he does not usually get a morning walk; instead, having the freedom to roam around my large garden.

Naturally, I could not have a visit from my Dutch relatives without my sister, Detta, and her husband, Richie, coming to visit too. We had a lovely Sunday together having a meal and a good catch up over the kitchen table. Because of Richie's mobility problems, Zig was not at home for them to witness his transformation. I chose to put him in kennels for the duration of their visit as I could not risk him being battered by Zig's killer tail. I was delighted when Andrew told Detta what a lovely, well behaved dog I have. I felt it was important for her to hear this as it was she who had been bitten on a previous visit in the early days. I was reminded again of how far we had come together.

Part Four: Looking Forward

Zig and I have been together for five years now and are moving to a smaller property with no stairs, located in the nearby town of Easingwold where the land is flatter and walks easier for me to manage. The move will be a bonus to my health needs.

Easingwold is a small market town at the foot of the Howardian Hills. It has three churches, Catholic, Protestant and Methodist, and one primary and one comprehensive school. The comprehensive school has recently become an academy for students from ages eleven to eighteen. The Galtres Centre is the main social meeting place for events and keep-fit. It also has a small well-stocked library which is run by volunteers. Parks are easy to come by, one of which boasts a bandstand where the local youth and adult brass bands entertain in the summer months; it is often the host for brass band competitions.

I will miss our old home and visiting some very special friends as often as I did. I will miss my garden and the changes in the land around there as the seasons roll by. I will not miss how dirty Zig can be when we get home.

Moving...

It seems my son forgot to take his belongings with him when he left home. My ex-husband and his wife have made two journeys of three hours each to collect his things to store in their garage. It is heavy work for them which is hindered by Zig's exuberance. We allow him a trip or two up and downstairs before putting him in the garden so that we can get on with the job in hand. He can come in again when the activity has settled down. They have worked hard and have a lot to take back with them. I offer them a rest and lunch which they refuse because they want to get back before dark.

Alice and Tom, plus friends from nearby are being more than helpful by transporting furniture from my house and garden to my new home over a cold and rainy February weekend.

Friends, Michael and Debbie, drive a 120-mile round trip to look after and walk Zig for me while I am still packing. He knows only too well that things are changing, and he is quiet and unsettled. Michael, Debbie and I are in the hall of a now nearly empty house talking small talk when I see Zig lying belly up in submission. I give him a tummy rub to ease his tension. He has never lain like this before and I feel for him.

The larger items such as wardrobes have been re-erected and put in place and the white goods are safely installed. I feel humbled by how hard my friends are working for me. I am reminded how much I will miss the village and the people I have grown to love, its walks and the ease of which it has been to call on friends.

Finally, it is done. We are in!

Before they go, Alice and Tom make sure I have a working television to keep me company and a bed made up for me to sleep in tonight. They leave me with a bottle of fizzy white wine.

Zig gets taken out in the rain for his first walk from this house. It feels strange to us both, but it works out well. However strange his new surroundings are, it has not spoilt his appetite. His feeding and water bowls now have a new place to stay, and he knows where they are already.

Wendy's husband drives her over here with a takeaway for us. We eat and chat amongst the piles of boxes and enjoy the wine before her husband calls to take her home.

Zig is staying close to me and is alert to every sound he hears. Eventually, grateful to my friends for making sure I have a made-up bed to sleep in, we fall asleep.

Getting settled...

When I wake up, I remember we now have a new home, with new neighbours and friends to meet, and new adventures to seek out. We have already met our next-door neighbour, Bill, and his dog.

I do not have an enclosed garden with this house. No more sleepily opening the back door to let Zig out while I make my first coffee of the day or waiting for him to let himself in before I go back to bed. I need to dress myself and fix his collar and lead on him before taking him out for his morning toilet break.

At the top of my list of priorities is to let the vets and insurance company know we have changed address.

Next, I inform the microchip company who cannot believe how quickly they are receiving the phone call from me. "Sometimes people leave it for too long before contacting us," my call handler tells me. I have been aware of this problem from watching television programmes where an animal has been lost or not been able to receive emergency treatment because of an owner's laxity in passing this information on. This was not going to happen to Zig.

Maybe it is because he has a new den to protect or maybe he just wants to keep me on my toes, but he has forgotten how to behave when people come to the door. He has decided it is time to bark loudly if anyone knocks on my front door. And if they cross the threshold, he is overzealous with his greetings. I have taped a notice to the letterbox which reads 'Dog in training- Please be patient'. I have also asked friends to help by calling in now and again, so I can get him to calm down before I open the door. His food is being delivered but he barks so ferociously, the delivery man will not wait for a signature. I tell him my dog is just a lot of noise, but he is not taking any chances.

This resurrected behaviour must stop. Again, he learns well with click and treat rewards. He still gives the obligatory bark to inform me of a visitor's approach, but he is much more settled, and visitors do not need to wait in the hallway before reaching the kitchen and being offered a cup of tea.

I call to talk to Bill next door and ask him about dog walking and if he wouldn't mind me joining him and his dog with Zig. I have not come far but do not know good dog walks around here. We arrange a twelve fifteen start. Our dogs meet. His is an older female who does not much like Zig's manners and lets him know about it.

Bill is a quiet man who has lived here for some time so knows all the places for dogs to sniff and stretch out. He leads the way for me as we do our first circuit together. I tell him about where I have moved from and my general history. He listens. I keep Zig on his lead as we walk through the housing estate. Already I am asking Bill where the livestock is. There are only sheep to consider on the routes we will take, and he will tell me where they will be. Once out of the estate and onto the crop fields I let Zig off his lead, making sure he does not run across them. They are not well established yet and the land is still wet. I can see sheep in the distance, but they are too far away as yet to be a worry, so I let him continue to sniff around this new land. He is trying to tease Bill's dog into playing, but being a good three years older, she is happily sniffing around and does not like having her peace disturbed. Once again, she lets him know she is unhappy with his behaviour.

"I know you only want to play Zig, but you need to have some manners around an older lady," I say. As if he understands what I have said, he returns to his own company. When the time is right, I put the lead back on him. It is obvious when he is aware of the sheep. I watch as he lifts his head higher above his shoulders. His ears are erect and turned forward. His pace is slow and intentional, and his tail stands out behind him. I say 'Leave'. He listens. I give him a treat. Remember the rules, his body relaxes but he is keeping his eyes on those sheep. I carry on with click and treat. He walks well going past them and once they are out of his sight, I let him run free again.

Once we are properly settled in our new home, I invite neighbours to share tea and cake. This ice-breaker does us all good and now they know who the new woman and her dog is.

It takes me well over a month to learn my way around the walks I am taken on, and without Bill's help, I know I would get lost. He chuckles at my inability to navigate, but I am becoming more comfortable with my surrounds now. I am aware Zig needs a lot more exercise than Bill's dog, so I have started making use of the local park, which I knew about before moving into the area.

It is good to meet up with friends again and watch the dogs play because there is no prey about. Knowing this helps me relax and allow myself to enjoy their play. Zig acts as though he has landed at his favourite holiday camp. He is suitably tired on the walk home and I am pleased he has been given the exercise he needs. I am able to navigate the area comfortably now, but I do have to remind myself where certain landmarks are.

A little problem...

It has been a long hard road to get us where we are, but I can now proudly say I have a lovely dog with a lovely personality. He is gentle, friendly, protective of me and loves to enthusiastically meet and greet people in the hope of a good rub around his ears or a treat. Sometimes he is still a little boisterous when he sees people he has not seen for a long time. I put that down to real love. He knows who his dog and people friends are and those who he has to wait for permission from before going to greet them. He sometimes has an 'I'll be back in a minute' attitude with his recall if he sees a special human or canine friend.

He will always be a high prey dog, but I can walk him with ease past anything while he is on his lead, and I know how much of a wide berth I must give him. I sometimes take him to fences with farm animals on the other side to remind him of the need for control before he gets a treat. He deserves treats more than ever at these times because he is going against all his innate instincts to hunt. I don't keep him near them for too long; just long enough to remind him of what is expected of him. He is very good at doing this now, and if I obey the rules, there is no trouble at all.

So, where's the problem in all this? We have a new home we are comfortable in, new neighbours who we are getting along with and new walks still to discover. Zig has a new girlfriend in the next-door neighbour's dog and is walking beautifully past the sheep.

Cats!

They are everywhere! Whereas they were a seldom sight in our old village, they are common here as people's companions and have no sense of danger around dogs. One cat seems to delight in teasing Zig as it sits comfortably on one of the patio chairs. Zig's response is to almost crash through the window to get at it. I know that in my near hysteria and mismanagement I will not have handled his outburst correctly, but I cannot remember how I dealt with it. I did know there was work to be done.

A friend has come to see me, and we take him out for a walk. We have barely left the house when we are passing a tall fence, on top of which, sits a cat. Do you remember me saying earlier I did not know dogs could jump so high? I do now! Zig is scaling the fence quicker than a Gladiator in competition. The only reason he does not get to the top is that I have him on his lead. There is no sign of the cat now, but it takes a moment or two until he realises any further efforts will be in vain.

At first, I was watchful for their presence when we were in the house but soon realised there was no need for my vigilance as his reaction was more than enough to let me know they were in the neighbourhood. His prey drive would be so heightened when he saw them, he would not know treats were being offered. Once I had his attention, it was easy to keep it while I had treats in my hand. As soon as his head would turn to look outside, I would click and treat until the offender had gone. I needed to have treats ready at all times. He knew I had to have them too, and if I was not quick enough, he would think he had a licence to once again demolish the house.

It had not taken too long a time before I could watch him at the point of poise and he would turn to me knowingly expecting a treat for not going after the cat. He always got one. Sometimes he would get as far as the bedroom door (only a short distance because I live in a bungalow) before remembering and would abruptly stop in his tracks. The thoughts in his head of 'Wait a minute. Good boy, good treats,' were clear. He would still like to get to them but there is far less drama now when he does.

On leaving the house, it was more important than it had been for a long time for him to wear his noseband and for me to keep an extra tight hold of his lead. I knew there were plenty of cats about but did not know when or where they were going to come out of hiding. I learnt to give parked cars a wide berth so he could not catch them from underneath. If I was caught unaware, he would wrench at my arm. The cats in this neighbourhood are particularly nonchalant in their attitude towards dogs, at times annoyingly daring as they saunter along or groom themselves in full view of Zig. They have no qualms in using my garden furniture to sunbath and stare into the windows while doing so. How is he supposed to cope with this? I had not had to work this hard with him since he saw the horses in their stables. I must have been close to the point of repetitive strain injury from the number of times I had to pull treats out of the bag to drop on the ground for him.

Whatever problems I had with him passing horses or sheep, at least I knew where they were. With cats, initially I would think once we had passed those we had seen, it would be a relatively calm walk, but no, one after another they would appear from elsewhere. Sometimes I would be stopped in my tracks in disbelieve when I saw them three, four or five lying together in a pride. Zig's natural reaction would be to charge, but with an ever-ready supply of treats to hand, we are both more in control now. He is willing to pass them by for a treat, and I am a more savvy lookout.

As with the horses and sheep, if he has a wide enough

berth, I can walk him past them with ease. He needs less of them these days and at times surprises me by hardly giving a cat a second glance. I never know the moment he might decide he has been good for long enough and have another go, but I am pleased with his progress and the ease with which I can walk him by them.

Cats apart, I am enjoying life in our new home, particularly the walks with Bill and his dog. Neighbours are friendly and willing to help when they can by doing odd jobs for me. I find older people have a more caring and sharing sense of community. I think the reason for this is they have lived through war when it is essential to help and look out for each other if their community is to survive. In turn, I like to help by doing the odd favour when I can.

We have only been at our new address a month when we have to visit the vets again. I was unaware Zig had a problem to the skin on the underside of his hind leg until he rolled and twisted on his back while stretching his legs in the air and I saw a wound near his groin area. Not being a new wound, I was to wonder again at the stoicism of these animals. He ate, drank and slept as normal. When we went out, he walked, ran or chased a ball. If he had not rolled over for me to see it when he did, he might have carried on coping with it and perhaps let it worsen as the days went by. If one of my children had done such a thing, I would have given them a cuddle and sympathy before cleaning the wound up and leaving them to it. With a dog, there are more concerns as they play in dirty places.

Options for treatment were given; naturally, I wanted the

best for him, but money, or lack of it, was a concern. I chose for him to have a week of antibiotic therapy and to clean the wound twice daily with tepid salt water. Zig was compliant to having the area bathed and took his medication without a problem. In a short time, the wound had healed. I think he may have been lucky though as it was looking a little sore and slightly infected when I discovered it.

We have found a new park near the school and straight away he is running over to meet the youth playing football. "Pick up your ball," I shout to them. They are quick to respond before their plaything has a puncture in it. Before I have time to apologise, they are playing with Zig and asking his name. He has now decided they are his new forever friends and takes little notice when I call him back to me. He has his own ball with him and I fight a losing battle as they throw it for him. He chases it and promptly brings it back for them to do it again. I have never taught him to fetch because I want to be walking rather than standing in a field waiting for him to come back to me, so I do not understand why he is doing it for them. One of them notices my ball thrower and soon I have a queue of them lining up to have a go at using it. Getting him to come to me when called once he spies them is still a challenge but is becoming easier as he is learning to take notice and they are learning not to throw his ball unless I say so.

In the same park, there is an old oak tree. Because of its great age, it is cordoned off by a low-level fence with a warning for people not to go beyond it because of the danger of falling branches. Zig ignores the notice and thoroughly enjoys going in there to sniff around, or to cool off as the area surrounding the tree is often overgrown by grass and wildflowers. He thinks this area belongs to him and he will chase other dogs out if they wander into its perimeter. Something else to work on but we are doing fine.

As the nights are growing longer, it is time again for Zig to wear his LED light coat. I chose to buy one of these because I am concerned lights on a collar around a dog's neck might be a little bright so close to their eyes. The lights from this coat form a large narrow U shape around the dogs back thereby lighting up more of the dog which makes it more visible from the back as well.

I get comments galore off people from, "That's a fancy jacket," and "I thought he was lit up like a reindeer for Christmas, but what a good idea," even a call of "That's totally sick," from an impressed and admiring youth. The best one though was from a slightly inebriated young woman, who when she saw us, stopped talking on her mobile and said, "Ooh, look, you've got a luminous dog." That made me smile most of all as she continued talking on her phone giving a great explanation to her listener of what was standing before her. She asked so many questions that I was wondering what the person she had left waiting on the other end of her call must have been thinking. After making much fuss of Zig, my luminous dog, and his jacket she gave me an uninhibited hug and a kiss on the cheek before going on her way, being guided home by the person on the other end of the phone.

Having given myself time to recuperate after the stresses of moving, I decided it was time to find some light voluntary work to keep me occupied and give a little help to my small area of society. I contacted our local community charity office and told them I was interested in becoming a member of their team. Days later, I was given an informal interview where I told them what I would be able and willing to do. It was decided I should join their befriending services. This simply means sitting with a client and keeping them company while their relative has a few hours of relief from caring or being company to a housebound person for a while. Zig would be allowed to join me if the clients were keen to meet him. This was good to know because we like to be together whenever we can. If I am going to leave him at home, he knows I am going out without him, so he lays stretched out of the floor while I kiss the top of his forehead goodbye. He has an 'Okay, see you later,' attitude when I do this. I do not leave him for too long and I know he is comfortable in his own company for a short while.

Another cat incident...

I am comfortable letting him run free in the fields if there are no sheep about. He knows his stops and will wait for me to reattach his lead.

This day he is waiting just out of sight. When I catch up with him, I see him looking down on a cat then swiftly moving his head out of the way while the cat strikes at him with open claws. My heart is in my mouth. "Zig come," I say. Unbelievably, he does. I praise and reward him.

Having reattached his lead, we go back to the cat. Obviously injured, the poor animal is unable to move from where it is. Bill has soon joined us, and we agree we should take the cat to the vet. Bill takes charge of Zig and his own dog while I take my cardigan off and wrap the cat inside and cradle it as we walk home. Bill has the harder job in handling two dogs. Before we get home, the cat dies. It is so upsetting; the only good is that it is now at peace.

Having left the dogs in their respective houses, Bill drives us to the vets. On the way, we speak about how clean and well looked after the cat is, and that there are no bite marks or saliva on it. I know Zig has not harmed it but cannot imagine what might have happened.

On arrival, Bill explains to the receptionist that we have a dead cat. We are sent through to a consultation room straight away where a vet is waiting for us. Once he has examined it and confirmed it deceased, he tells us that from looking at the injuries to its hindquarters, it had most likely been run over by a car. As bad as this news was, I did feel some relief at the confirmation my dog had not attacked it.

We wait while the vet checks for a microchip identity of this cat that looked so well cared for. We watch and wait for a beep as the scanner is passed over its body, hoping, though not looking forward to it, to at least be able to let the owners know what has happened. Sadly, there is no microchip. All we can hope for is that its owner telephones the vet practices around the area or puts an advert in the local advertiser. I call in at the vets a few days later to ask if anyone had been asking after it. Sadly, there have been no enquiries made. Nor are there any advertisements in the local advertiser or shop windows asking of its whereabouts.

More new friends…

I had learned from a local dog walking group of a new family to the area who had adopted a rescue dog and were having difficulties socialising him with other dogs, as he bit them on meeting. When I met him, I found him to be a very handsome Dalmatian in his prime, and very good with people and dogs he knew. These people knew how to network and informed other dog walkers that they had an unruly dog in training and were working hard at getting their new charge to meet and greet other dogs properly. This was such a wise thing to do and I wondered why I had not thought to do such a sensible thing when I adopted Zig.

I first met his owner, Suri, while walking Zig in the local park. I had guessed who she was from the description she had put on the dog walkers' site. We hit it off immediately while our dogs sorted themselves out. Once they had agreed on a compatible relationship between themselves and Suri had given me many apologies, we had our first of many meetups and dog walks together. It has been an inspiration watching her dog respond to training and learning not to bite others when he meets them.

With the help of friends, we walked lots more rural routes with our dogs. Sheep were often a problem when we decided to do so, which meant stopping and doubling back in order to avoid them. I had to do something about this, otherwise, we were never going to complete an intended circuit.

It was when walking with Bill and his dog the day came when I said to him, "If we go through that field will you keep an eye on us and help out if needed?"

"Aye, alright," he said. Bill's answers are always short and to the point. With Zig's noseband in situ and treats at the ready, I held on tightly to his lead before starting our way across the sheep-packed field. Wow! What has happened to my dog? His lead walking and behaviour around his second favourite prey was impeccable. He watched them with every step we took but made no attempt to lunge. Treats being a good enough exchange for a possible hearty meal. One or two sheep did start running towards us, perhaps hoping for some grain, which did get his hackles up a little, but he was easily calmed with a 'Leave it,' from me. The walk across the field was amazingly uneventful. Bill and I were left only to wonder as we enjoyed the rest of our walk.

Christmas is not a good time for me, but friends do their best to make it so. 2017 was to be different because David and Karina and my grandson, Mateo, were coming to stay. This would be Mateo's third Christmas and it would be more fun than ever.

We are spending the day with David's father and his wife. There has never been any animosity between us. This is a late invite, so I have a great problem in getting Zig housed for the day because everywhere is booked up. I suggest they go and leave me here with Zig. But no, that won't do, so Zig is packed into the boot of my ex's car and we leave for Lancashire.

On Christmas morning, Mateo cannot contain his excitement. He has so many gifts to unwrap; he does not finish unwrapping one before he goes on to the next. Adults join in the festivity, enjoying his delight and exchanging our own gifts. David and his Dad put themselves in charge of cooking the dinner while the ladies tidy up from Christmas morning and set the table. There are three dogs, including Zig, sharing Christmas with us and they get on well. They are not left out of the celebrations and enjoy their own Christmas dinner too.

We have some snow this year and, coming from Peru, it is a new experience for Mateo. He is not unhappy about our cold weather even having come from a hot climate. He loves Zig and plays with him as much as he can and gets great pleasure at throwing a ball from its thrower and watching the dog run after it. There are plenty of deep puddles to watch him roll or swim in, and Mateo laughs when Zig comes back to us drenched in mud. "Sig, Sig," he calls to him.

I think David and Karina are impressed with the transformation in Zig's behaviour and quickly see he will be safe with their son. I have no doubt about how he will behave. On this occasion, it has not been my dog who has given me pleasure, but my grandson as he has learnt to socialise and care for an animal. He loves 'Sig', as he calls him, and looks forward more to him visiting Peru than he does me. I will forgive him because of his young age.

Village life...

It is spring, and the good people of Easingwold are tending to their gardens. Being a fair weathered gardener, I am not quite ready to make a start yet, but I feel an obligation to keep my patch looking good. I go ahead picking out weeds that have already started to invade the flower beds and pot plants. The soil is still wet making it hard to pull them out. Fortunately the snowdrops, crocuses, daffodils and hyacinths are hiding them well.

Zig loves to sit outside and watch me gardening. The only thing disturbing his leisure are the cats that pass by. This disturbs me too as I leave what I am doing to quieten him. He behaves well now when I take him out and we pass them by on his lead, but when it comes to them invading his own territory, he is worse than an impatient driver behind the wheel of a car.

I am pleased we are coming to the end of the wet season and look forward to not having to scrub Zig clean before we get indoors again. However, we are not there yet.

Suri and her husband Ben have come to take Zig and me to a small dog show just outside town. Their dog, the one they had so much trouble with when they first adopted him, won first prize for being the most handsome dog in the show, which was no surprise, and I was pleased for them.

The agility circuit gave us the best fun of all. Before starting our round, I asked the leader if I could take Zig off the lead. Before I did so, I told him Zig was a novice, but he said it was still fine. We made our start, and as if he was a born professional Zig jumped jumps, climbed frames, crossed long bars, jumped through hoops and, after a little persuasion, ran through the tunnels.

"You told me he was a novice," the leader said.

"Honestly he has only ever done this once about five years ago," I replied.

"Well, he's clearly remembered it."

After entering a few more competitions which he did not

do well at, not even for showing the judges how clever he is at opening and closing doors, we returned to the agility circuit. I was looking forward to him bettering his earlier performance when, as if to tell the world he indeed was a novice, he jumped over every obstacle in sight. If they were too long to jump over, he went at them width ways and did it that way. The tunnels too were not to be run through anymore as he jumped over them like a horse at Beecher's Brook.

Summer...

This summer is a hot one and people and animals are finding it hard to cope. I try to keep Zig cool in any way I can, but it isn't easy. As eager as he is to get outside, he cannot last long in the heat of the daytime sun. We are doing our long walk no earlier than eight in the evening when the rays are less harsh. It is stressful watching his efforts to cool off as he pants hard and tires himself out doing so. Throughout the nights, he wakes several times in response to the heat and pants again. I can feel the effort he is putting into it and wish I could do something to aid his sleep. A cool air fan is in situ, but he does not know to benefit from it unless I guide him to the best position to feel the cool air. Outside I have set up a paddling pool of cool water, but he avoids it, perhaps thinking it is bath time. I leave it for a couple of days making no effort to call him to it, hoping he will realise he can trust it, but he is not convinced. I stand in it with treats in my hand to try and coax him in. The best I can do is get him to put one paw in the water so that he can get his reward. I put his collar and lead on him and have him put all four paws into the pool. He does not sit down, but I think it is at least helping to cool his body temperature a little. This weather is purgatory for him indoors or outdoors. Even though I am dreading the winter for myself, I wish it on for him.

The lack of rain and the scorching hot sun has taken its toll on the land. Because it so is dry the farmers are having to work harder at keeping fields watered to reap a good crop. Their livestock having to be further catered for because of the effects of the heat too. Garden grass and public verges are yellow-brown instead of the usual lush green. Surprisingly, there is no official drought in this area so people are watering their flower borders and pots early morning and late evening keeping colour to their surroundings. Somehow the trees manage to keep themselves looking well and I am particularly impressed at the Hawthorn this year. Its berries change from white to orange-red and keep blooming well into the autumn.

I enjoy watching the bees at the lavender either side of my back door while Zig is trying to spar with next doors dog. He cannot reach her as his lengthy tether is not quite long enough. I am such a friend of the bees these past years and worry about their dwindling numbers and what the loss of them would do to our planet. Where would we be without them in our food chain? No berries, no cherries, no honey for us or the birds and other animals around us that rely on these foodstuffs to keep healthy. Where would we be without their ability to pollinate our land for us? Crops would not grow, flowers would be no more. Picture this desolation if you can.

New housing is being built on a lot of the land people have previously used for walking their dogs; we have to look harder for places where our dogs can stretch their legs. The sad thing for them is having to be kept on their leads for more time when they should be playing. I am sure not by intent, but the builders have conveniently made a sizeable soil hill outside the perimeters of one of the sites. Bigger dogs such as Zig take to this unintended gift and enjoy digging their way through it as they are making their way to the top. This gives them an extra ten minutes playtime we were not expecting them to get. In typical dog fashion, they quickly adapt, and in their own ways let us know they are happy just as long as they have us for company and protection.

Once again, I have cause to worry about finances and am wondering how I will manage to feed my dog. As if an angel from heaven has been listening to my thoughts, friends Kim and Leslie have arrived with a bag of food for Zig refusing to accept payment. How lucky can one girl be?

Volunteering...

Because of my lack of transport, the voluntary carers organisation had only one client for me to sit with and there were no potential new customers on their books. I was wondering where else I could be useful when I learnt of a Christian Coffee Shop soon to be opening within walking distance of my home. This new venture was to be run by a husband and wife team. I met the lady while walking past the premises and told her what I was hoping to do. Having been given a time to call back when I would be likely to find her husband at work, I made sure I would be passing at the right time to meet him. I met him at the front of the shop and explained I had been talking to his wife earlier and had come to ask if I could be any use as a volunteer for a few hours a week working front of house. I explained my health limitations, what I felt I would be able to do and that I would not be able to do any more than two hours a day twice a week. A few weeks later, I was part of their voluntary team working the hours I wanted. As before, Zig would stretch out on the floor as I was leaving with that, 'Okay, I know I'm not going anywhere, I'll wait for you to get back,' look, while he allowed me to give him his kiss on his forehead goodbye.

An ongoing battle...

All was going smoothly until I was attacked by another bout of disability and once again, I was finding it hard to look after myself and was worrying about Zig's care.

Even though the land is flatter here, I felt it was all too much of a struggle to look after him properly. Again, I contacted local and national dog walking charities in the hope he could be given a good hour walk each day. Again, no luck. Feeling worried about Zig and desperate for myself, I put an advert in the local advertiser, as if worded by Zig, asking for help with his walks until I got better. In the meantime, Suri offered to put an advert in the local dog walkers' site via Facebook for me. In less than a day I had five walkers willing to walk him free of charge. Once the local advertiser was published, I had a further two willing walkers to add to my list of helpers. One day per week, hail, rain or shine they each call to collect him and give him a good walk. He has bonded with them all and they with him. They look forward to the extra special greeting he has for them when they arrive. They are true heroes to me whose time and generosity is appreciated more than they could know.

I also cut back on the time I could volunteer at the coffee shop, only being able to offer help if they could provide transport there and back for me as walking is too much of a strain and I am feeling more breathless. Even then, I cannot always guarantee I can help. I hate to let them down, but some days I just cannot be of help and have no choice but to bow out of my usual offers of help. There is never a moment's complaint, even when I let them down at short notice. Instead, I am always told not to worry and how much they appreciate what I do.

Wanting to build up my strength up again, I asked one of the dog walkers if Zig, Wendy and I could walk a little way with her. We managed a slow walk to a small park where Zig was let off the lead. Because we had no ball to throw, he picked up a small piece of stick to play with. Before it could be taken from him, he had managed to get it lodged between his teeth across the bridge of his upper palate. Seeing what he had done, I tried to remove it, but it was stuck fast. I knew he needed to be taken to the vets, and walking there was the only option, but already he was showing signs of distress. I tried to dislodge it a few more times on our way, but it was not going to be moved. He was walking as best he could while shaking his head or using his paws to try and dislodge it.

With me being unwell and struggling with mobility, Zig, Wendy and the dog walker reached the surgery ahead of me. I was so exhausted by the time I arrived, all I could do was sit on the floor of the consultation room and try to regain my breath. I felt light headed with fatigue. While waiting for the vet's arrival, Zig managed to expel the offending stick from his mouth. What a relief! He was given the all clear by the vet and once I had regained my strength, we slowly walked home.

More treatment...

Zig has not been walking well recently so it is time to take him back to the vets. This time he has injured his cruciate ligament. These ligaments cross over each other and are attached to the upper end of the lower tibia (shin) bones which in turn are attached to the bottom of the longer femur (thigh) bones of each leg and are hidden behind the kneecap. He goes in for his operation on a Monday morning and will take up to three months for him to regain full use of his leg again. Exercise will initially be very limited, increasing as his post-operative condition improves. I feel for him being such an active dog needing to be restricted like this and worry he will go stir crazy. However, I know all will be well in the end and it will be me who is left to remember the worry I had about his convalescence. At least I know he will not be pulling on his lead for a while. Curtains will be kept closed during the daytime to hide cats from his view and stop him from charging around the house ruining the results of the operation he has needed. Being unleashed indoors he is not as well behaved in controlling his prey drive as he is when we are outdoors. He will be banned from jumping on furniture, and I have borrowed a cage which I have padded out for his comfort, so he won't feel the need to jump up on the soft furnishings. He will not be kept in it for long periods. Little deeds like these are a sensible and small price to pay for success. He is six years old now and showing little sign of growing old despite the treatments he has sometimes needed on his many visits to his friends at the vets.

On the morning of the procedure, I am awake before the streets are aired and get him to the vets in plenty of time. Zig is given a quick examination to check he is suitable for surgery before pre-operation questions are asked and answered, and I sign the consent form. That done, he is taken from me and taken into the pre-operation room. I become emotional, not because I am worried about his operation's success, but because he goes in with the innocence of a newborn baby.

After the operation, I get a well-informed courtesy call from the vet who operated. I am told how worthwhile the surgery was because she had also found a tear to one of his menisciscuses. These act as shock absorber pads when moving the legs at the knees, especially if walking or running. The procedure has gone well, and Zig is now sleeping off the anaesthetic. He will stay overnight.

The following morning, I receive a call with an update on his condition. He is doing well, eating and drinking and already weight bearing on the affected leg. These animals are amazing. I can take him home that afternoon providing I can get a willing neighbour to provide transport for us. I call on Bill who is as willing as ever to lend a hand and will take me to collect him at three-thirty.

I can hardly wait to have him home again knowing he has

come through another procedure well. I promise myself I will follow all the post-operative instructions to the letter so he will be able to run freely again sooner.

Bill and I wait at reception for Zig's arrival. Five minutes later he is brought out to us sporting a large Buster collar. Already, he is walking well, and with tail wagging, he hurries as best he can to make contact with me again. Once he is sure he has got me back for keeps, he turns his attention to Bill who is as gentle in his greeting to Zig as he always is. The young vet gives me post-operative advice, asks if he has anti-inflammatory medications at home, which he does, gives me antibiotic medication for him, reminding me he must complete the course and goes over the do's and don'ts of post-operative rehabilitation.

Zig is eager to jump into the back seat of the car. I make sure he does not do this, though it is a difficult job lifting his back legs in. Helping him out when we arrive home is much easier. Once indoors, he checks on his food and water bowls before I take him for a toilet break. Watching the lengthy stream of urine flowing from him I don't think he can have emptied his bladder properly since yesterday morning. He quickly settles down. People are texting and phoning to ask how he is. I am pleased to tell them the news is good. He eats only half of his normal food allowance at teatime but takes his medications well.

The cage I have borrowed for him, though having ample room to rest in for a while, is not large enough to allow him to move around in and stretch out properly. I know if I go to bed, he will follow me and jump up which he must not do. I decide to sleep next to him on the sofa. I have folded a double duvet and covered it with an old sheet for him to lay on and I prepare to sleep beside him.

That night is a nightmare for him. His pain is causing pathetic whimpering which continues throughout the night. I feel helpless not being able to do anything to alleviate it for him as he works at repositioning his limbs to find some comfort. Sleep is fitful for both of us. I am relieved for him when he can have his next dose of analgesia (painkilling medication). Breakfast is sparse, but again he takes his medications well.

Wendy comes to stay on the Wednesday and he is so delighted to see her it seems he has forgotten his pain for now. We are due to sit with a gentleman as part of the befriending services, but I will not be going. Today I will stay with Zig. It would be cruel to leave him, and I would worry about him if I wasn't here. Wendy returns with our evening meal at five-thirty. Once again Zig has forgotten his pain on seeing her. As the evening progresses his pain lessens, and he is much more settled.

When it is time for bed, Wendy goes to sleep in the bedroom. Zig does not like this. Whenever she comes to stay his loyalties to me are abandoned and he always chooses to sleep next to her. Thankfully, she is quickly asleep and does not hear him whimpering in protestation at not being in with her. That night is a nightmare for me.

He eats a good breakfast the next morning and drinks plenty of water. The Buster collar he is wearing is proving to be as big a pain as his operation site as he bashes it into every object he walks past. He is even having difficulties getting through the door spaces, ruining my recently painted woodwork. Only one thing for it, he decides to start walking backwards to avoid crashing into things. This dog just gets cleverer.

Bill takes us for his post-operative check-up and all the signs are good. Though he did jump into the car on our journey to the vets, this has done no harm. Stitches are to be taken out in a week.

I am taking him out for five-minute walks three times a day which is enough time for him to empty his bladder and bowels and have a little sniff around. I think he has forgotten he has had an operation as he is already pulling on his lead. What was that I said earlier about knowing he wouldn't be pulling for a while? I need to put his noseband on again even though we are only going for short walks, but it is good for him to have his Buster collar off for a while.

I need to leave him at home so I can buy a few groceries. I will be as quick as I can and hope he does not jump on the sofa. I have nothing but myself to block his access to this so hoping is all I can do. As I am returning, I see two youths. As I pass, one of them calls out, "How is your dog?" I had not realised there was such interest in him. I thank the boy for his concern and let him know things are improving. I feel heartened by him.

Less than a week later, Zig is obviously in less pain and trying to jump up on the sofa. I stop him from doing so by laying across it and he gets the message. There is plenty more to jump on though, so I corral him in by putting obstacles across chairs and doors.

His Buster collar is not the deterrent it is meant to be as he can still lick his wound. So, I give him relief from it while I am with him. Unfortunately, my brain is in a muddle due to fibro fog (this is forgetfulness as part of the condition of fibromyalgia) and I have forgotten to put it on him before I go out. I have also forgotten to barricade the bedroom door. When I return, he has opened the door to the bedroom and is on the bed having taken one of his stitches out and has had a go at another one. Fortunately, he is to have them out in two days so I do not think there is much harm done. I will have to let the vet decide.

I am tired after my time out and decide to put his collar back on him, so I do not need to worry about him getting at any more stitches while I have a nap. Before sleeping, I go to the kitchen to make a cup of coffee to quench my thirst. When I get back into the front room, I look at him and find I have put the collar on back to front and he is looking at me while wearing it like a cape. No deterrent from getting at his stitches with it on that way around. I laugh out loud at my stupidity, and because I have a big mouth, I share this faux pas with friends.

It is Thursday and time to have his stitches taken out. I have noticed the top two areas of stitching are looking a little red but hope for the best. At one o'clock Bill is waiting for me. I get into the car with Zig. Bill and I are talking about the possibility of new gas central heating to the area soon. But the journey is short, so we do not have time to say much about it. It is not long before I am called in for Zig's appointment. I tell the vet about what happened when I found him on the bed having taken a suture out because I had forgotten to put his Buster collar on. She examines the wound and lets me know the top of it is slightly infected and swollen so only the lower stitches will be taken out today. Bang goes my hope of letting him keep the collar off. I am told he is to wear it until the remaining stitches come out next Tuesday. In the meantime, if I feel any signs of hardening of the swollen area or see any weeping from it, he is to return to the vets straight away. Now I feel guilty for being so forgetful in putting the collar on before I go out. He is put on a course of antibiotic tablets.

The autumn leaves in their variegated colours are covering the ground making crisp rustling sounds underneath our footsteps. The end of Zig's nose is hidden in their depth as he investigates what is underneath. The deciduous trees are now mostly bare, and birds' nests are looking abandoned and forlorn without their leafy coverage. I am pleased I have tended to my garden. The ceanothus, honeysuckle and lavender have all been cut back, and most of the flowering pots have been emptied or cut back to make way for autumn and winter plants such as the clematis, pansies, phormiums and sedums.

Because Zig loves this weather, he enjoys his time lounging or pacing in the garden or watching me as I work. Sometimes even better, is the attention he gets from neighbours who he now considers lifelong friends. There is never any chance they will not know he is there as he loudly vocalises his desperation to see them by his excited, 'Please come and play, I haven't seen you for ages,' whining. Or maybe he will give one or two barks as if to say; 'Hey I am over here'. Any time outside in this weather is alright by him.

The night temperature is considerably cooler, and I am noticing the absence of hedgehogs. I am sad about this. When I moved to Easingwold, I was pleased to see they are quite prolific here and enjoy watching them foraging in the gardens. It gives me hope for the future of these innocuous, endangered mammals, just so long as there are not so many houses to be built or fake lawns to be laid to deny them of their habitat. I am happy that Zig has no interest in them. Perhaps they are too slow moving for him to consider them prey.

Taking him for a short walk is difficult with the collar on, which because of its size is getting in the way of his sniffing the ground and makes a harsh scraping sound as he walks along. When on the grass it acts as a digger pulling it up with the top layer of soil. It is autumn now, so he is also left with a scoopful of leaves to carry around. He is going stir crazy and jumping up at the front door handle begging to be let out. I do not know if is worse for him jumping up at the door handle as he tries to open the door so often or going for extra short walks.

Finally, it's Tuesday and the remaining stitches are coming out this afternoon. The vet is pleased with the look of the scar today, so the job is done, and he can be free of the Buster collar.

I am advised to increase the length of his walks by five minutes per week. I am happy with this. I hope Zig is too.

Now we are home again, and he is free to move from room

to room without the bother of the collar and does not need to walk backwards to get around anymore. Too late for the paintwork. I will have to do some serious touching up where the Buster collar has scraped it away. All there is left to see now is his scar, but already the hair is growing well. By this time next month, there will be no sign of it.

He is healing very well, and I have increased his walking time gradually as the vets have advised. Keeping him on his lead has been a chore for both of us and letting him loose from it is another gradual process. The first time I do, it is only for a minute or two at night, so he can do his toileting in peace and untethered when there is nothing around to excite him. He has more and more freedom as each week goes by and it is good to see him walking pain-free.

Having his exercise restricted has been difficult for him to tolerate and it has shown in his behaviour. If a visitor called, he demanded attention, showing them that he wanted to play games to vent his frustration. When he didn't get what he wanted, he reverted to destruction, pulling the stuffing out of pillows or chewing at shoes. Thankfully, all this is behind him again and he is back to normal. He is still greeting visitors enthusiastically but settles down quickly. He never will be a dog who sits quietly in a corner when a friend calls, but that's part of his charm.

I have been for another wonderful holiday, staying with David and Karina, and have better established a loving relationship with my grandson Mateo.

Zig has holidayed with the staff at his favourite kennels where he knows and loves them all. I have been kept updated with videos of him having the best of times. I can see he has been very happy, but I have missed him so very much.

It was a magical time when he was brought home. He stormed through the front door and jumped up to greet me (I forgave him this once after such a long absence from each other). He wanted to let me know how happy he was to have me back again before checking that everything was as per usual in his home.

Now we are back to our normal routine and it is lovely to go out walking with Bill and his dog again.

We are enjoying our seventh winter together, but the weather is so unseasonal it is more like spring. Lawns are already being cut and catkins are hanging in abundance from hazelnut trees. There are already signs of nuts beginning to develop. Even the heather is in early bloom.

Zig can now run freely chasing after a ball or playing with other dogs having done his full postoperative rehab. He is enjoying every moment life has to offer him. Long may he continue.

Hope...

He is beside me enjoying a peaceful sleep after his afternoon walk. His presence helps keep the house warm and occupied. Without him, it would feel cold and empty. I am blessed with a loving family and friends who make sure I am never alone for too long. But Zig provides that extra warmth when they are not here, or there for a chat at the other end of the telephone.

When I first adopted him, I thought it was me coming to

the rescue with all I had to offer him. But this is not exactly true. He has rescued me in so many ways; giving me the impetus to carry on in times of ill health or disability. Because I love him and know he needs caring for, it helps me soldier on. But I am grateful to the people who relieve me from the stresses of walking him when it is all too much.

I wonder what our next significant episode will be. Whatever it is, we should have many more happy years together. I have kept him through thick and thin as I have always sworn to do. I knew the moment I saw him I had fallen in love with him, reprobate though he was, and whatever challenges lay ahead, I would take great care of him and be the most responsible dog owner I could be. I have made mistakes, and there have been times I have been close to tears, others have too, over his behaviour but we have come through it all with positive results. I am not pretending I have changed a devil into an angel. (Well I have almost).

I am sure I saved him from certain death had I returned him to the RSPCA because of his biting and prey drive. I am proud and delighted at what we have achieved together over these issues, and for all the other training we have succeeded in.

I did not know how hard and rewarding our journey would be. Despite our difficult times together I have never regretted my decision to adopt Zig. I hope you have enjoyed reading about our journey together. I have certainly enjoyed sharing it with you.

Cinnamon Trust

In this book, I have spoken about contacting animal charities when I needed them. It is unfortunate they have not been able to help because of lack of volunteers in the area. I am particularly thinking about the Cinnamon Trust. This registered charity helps provide care for small animals like dogs and cats of elderly (over 60 years old) or terminally ill people. Volunteers help with dog walking, feeding animals, looking after a pet while owners are at hospital appointments etc., or fostering a family pet(s) while the owner is in hospital. If the owner sadly dies or needs to go into full-time care, they will re-home their pet. I wish my own health was stable enough to volunteer for them, but I cannot be relied upon. There are other dog walking charities, who will do an equally wonderful job, but those I have contacted only work within a certain area. The Cinnamon Trust is a nationwide charity who rely on the support of their volunteers and subscriptions where possible. All they ask for is your time, and there are no costs to the person needing help or those who take on any charges. Please consider helping if you can.

They can be contacted on 01736 757 900. Or by post to The Cinnamon Trust, 10, Market Square, Hayle, Cornwall TR27 4HE.

Bonfire Night Plea

Taking Zig for a walk in November, I met a man who usually has two dogs with him.

"Why only one dog?" I asked.

"The other one died on Bonfire Night", he tells me. Then he unfolds the entire horror story.

Both his dogs were afraid of fireworks. Knowing this, he took them out for their walk early so he would have them back home before the night's events. Unfortunately, a rather loud banger was set off early, resulting in one dog taking such fright he bolted and entangled himself in a barbed wire fence. The poor dog was in such distress he further entangled itself in the barbs. The tragic result of this dog's fear and pain was euthanasia. If the dog's life had been saved, it would have been minus three of his limbs. What an appalling incident, and all for the sake of fireworks.

I understand it is a celebration enjoyed by many, but please let us enjoy this occasion at a licensed only event at a nationally agreed time on one evening of each year and agree to a ban the selling of fireworks to anyone other than legitimate event marshals. Perhaps this way such tragedies and injuries to people and animals will be reduced, and hopefully stopped.

Recommendations

The Dutch House Art Cafe, Contemporary Art Gallery and wildlife gardens and park. A lovely spacious dog-friendly place to eat and browse, set between Crayke and Brandsby, York. 01347 889431

Morning Coffee and Afternoon Tea, Easingwold. A spacious charity run cafe with a varied menu and super friendly staff. 01347 821692